From Me to

With this practical book, you'll learn effective ways to engage students in reading and writing by teaching them narrative nonfiction. By engaging adolescents in narrative, literary, or creative nonfiction, they can cultivate a greater understanding of themselves, the world around them, and what it means to feel empathy for others. This book will guide you to first structure a reading unit around a narrative nonfiction text, and then develop lessons and activities for students to craft their own personal essays. Topics include:

- Engaging your students in the reading of a nonfiction narrative with collaborative chapter notes, empathy check-ins, and a mini research paper to deepen students' understanding;
- Helping your students identify meaningful life events, recount their experiences creatively, and construct effective opening and closing lines for their personal essays;
- Encouraging your students to use dialogue, outside research, and a clear plot structure to make their narrative nonfiction more compelling and polished.

The strategies in this book are supplemented by examples of student work and snapshots from the author's own classroom. The book also includes interviews with narrative nonfiction writers MK Asante and Johanna Bear. The appendices offer additional tips for using narrative nonfiction in English class, text and online resources for teaching narrative nonfiction, and a correlation chart between the activities in this book and the Common Core Standards.

Jason Griffith is a National Board Certified teacher and a National Writing Project Fellow who taught middle and high school English for 12 years in Carlisle, PA. He is currently a Teaching Associate and PhD Student (English Education) at Arizona State University and an Adjunct Instructor at Pennsylvania State University, Harrisburg.

From Me to We

Using Narrative Nonfiction to Broaden Student Perspectives

Jason Griffith

Routledge
Taylor & Francis Group

NEW YORK AND LONDON

First published 2017
by Routledge
711 Third Avenue, New York, NY 10017

and by Routledge
2 Park Square, Milton Park, Abingdon, Oxon, OX14 4RN

Routledge is an imprint of the Taylor & Francis Group, an informa business

Library of Congress Cataloging-in-Publication Data
Names: Griffith, Jason, author.
Title: From me to we : using narrative nonfiction to broaden student
    perspectives / by Jason Griffith.
Description: New York : Routledge, [2017] | Includes bibliographical
    references.
Identifiers: LCCN 2016015150 | ISBN 9781138185029 (hardback) |
    ISBN 9781138185036 (pbk.) | ISBN 9781315644790 (e-book)
Subjects: LCSH: Narration (Rhetoric)—Study and teaching
    (Secondary) | Creative nonfiction—Study and teaching
    (Secondary) | English language—Composition and exercises—
    Study and teaching (Secondary)
Classification: LCC LB1631 .G766 2017 | DDC 808/.0420712—dc23
LC record available at https://lccn.loc.gov/2016015150

ISBN: 978-1-138-18502-9 (hbk)
ISBN: 978-1-138-18503-6 (pbk)
ISBN: 978-1-315-64479-0 (ebk)

Typeset in Palatino
by Apex CoVantage, LLC

Printed and bound in the United States of America by Publishers Graphics, LLC on sustainably sourced paper.

For Dr. Sue F. Johnson

Contents

Meet the Author

Jason Griffith is a Teaching Associate and PhD Student (English Education) at Arizona State University. A National Board Certified Teacher and Fellow of the National Writing Project, Jason taught middle school and high school English for 12 years in Carlisle, PA. In 2012, Jason received NCTE's Edwin A. Hoey Award for Outstanding Middle Level Educator, and he currently serves on NCTE's Middle Level Section Steering Committee.

Jason has presented at numerous national and regional conferences, and his work has been published in the *Language Arts Journal of Michigan* as well as collected volumes published by the International Society of Technology in Education (ISTE) and Rowman & Littlefield. Jason also has written for *Hippocampus Magazine*, the Nerdy Book Club, *Talking Writing*, and the Pennsylvania Council of the Teachers of English Language Arts (PCTELA) blog.

Jason's research interests include English Education, Secondary Writing Instruction, Narrative/Creative/Literary Nonfiction, Music in the English Language Arts, Student Participatory Media, and Contemplative Pedagogy. Visit Jason's website and blog at www.breathedeepandteach.com and follow him on Twitter @JGriff_Teach.

Acknowledgements

This is my first book and, as such, it fulfills a lifelong dream to contribute a volume to the world's library. I owe many thanks.

First, as this is a book for teachers, I would have nothing to contribute to such an audience if it weren't for my students, many of whom are featured in the pages of this book, and some are even cited in the reference list. I thank all of you for being willing to try each of my ideas, some more zany than others, and I cannot tell you how much I value the trust you all demonstrated through your brave writing and honest discussion. Each time I searched through your work for quotes and samples to share, I reflected on our time together, and I smiled. Special thanks to my lunch bunch for the extra work you put in and for reading early drafts of some chapters from this book. I will always appreciate your humor and your candor.

Next, thank you to the best graphic designer I know: my wife Kelly. You turned my scribbled ideas into coherent charts and illustrations that add so much to this book. We make a great team, and I'm lucky to know you! I encourage readers to check out more of Kelly's art and design at www.kellygriffithart.com

Also, immense thanks to the generous writers who contributed to this project.

MK Asante, the first time I heard you speak you said that "talking to writers makes a difference in the quality of the conversation." I agree completely, and I'm so grateful that you contributed to our conversation. I know that your own students at Morgan State are fortunate and must enjoy every class (which I imagine is filled with stories, film, rap, laughter, and maybe even some tears). Everyone should not only read MK's amazing memoir *Buck* but also head to mkasante.com to download the *Buck* soundtrack and to check out some of MK's other writing, film, and music.

Johanna Bear, I can always say that I knew you *when*, but the first year I knew you, you won a national gold key in the Scholastic Art and Writing Awards and were selected for publication in *The Best Teen Writing* as an eighth grader, so it's a lofty *when*, and you've continued to build on it impressively. It's been a humbling privilege to watch you work your tail off to grow and improve as a writer. Thank you for contributing your wisdom to this project so that other student writers can aspire to follow in your footsteps. I look forward to many great things ahead for you in college and beyond.

Steve Lopez, thank you not only for writing the book and columns that my students read for our narrative nonfiction unit featured in this book, but thank you for taking the time to videoconference with us. It's an experience that none of us will soon forget, and we continue to learn a lot from you and Nathaniel through your work.

To my parents and past English teachers, thank you for supporting me and teaching me to love writing and reading, which paved the way for me loving to teach writing and reading. I wouldn't be me without you.

Kathi Bletz, thank you for being open to including a narrative nonfiction unit in our tenth grade curriculum and for scrounging money to buy copies of new books during a time of tight budgets. You were a receptive and supportive department chair, and I continue to appreciate your work in that capacity.

Also, a huge round of thanks to Lauren Davis and the rest of the folks at Routledge Eye on Education. You were quite patient with me as I moved cross-country, started a doctoral program, and I stretched the timeline to complete this book by months. From the many extensions to incorporating Kelly's design into the cover art, I am grateful to work with you for my first book, and I hope we work together on more in the future.

Finally, I dedicate this book to the memory of Dr. Sue F. Johnson, my professor and mentor during my student teaching at the Indiana University of Pennsylvania. Your reputation intimidated me when I first took a class from you as a sophomore, and when you were assigned as my student teaching supervisor, I knew you'd be tough. You didn't disappoint in that regard, but it also didn't take me long to learn how much you cared that I become the best teacher I could be. I am convinced I would not be the teacher I am today without your guidance during my pre-service. You passed just as I began my own doctoral work in English Education. As I hope to one day have the same impact on future teachers that you had on me, I remember you, and I thank you.

Introduction

From Me to We: Broadening Millennial Minds through Narrative Nonfiction

Millennials are selfish, right?

Take, for instance, a former student who visited during my planning period a few weeks ago. "How's it going, Mr. G?" was her only catch-up question before she jumped to her true purpose. "So, I'm doing the Polar Bear Plunge again. Want to make a donation?" Despite this being the first time I'd seen this particular student all year, I dug out a ten dollar bill because the event supported a good cause, The Special Olympics.

For the next 20 minutes, she filled me in on her plan to become a nurse. First, she'd complete an internship with a local hospital during her senior year, and then she'd train to become a Certified Nursing Assistant in order to be able to work in the field while also working through a college RN program. Her mom was really proud, she said, especially because her older siblings were still figuring out their post-high school lives. Then, a glance at the clock prompted an "I'd better get going. Bye!"

No questions about my current classes or my family, no reminiscing about the memorable lessons she'd enjoyed as a student in my eighth grade English class or the conversations we'd shared 2 years later when she was assigned to my tenth grade study hall. Just a quick raid on my wallet and a self-indulgent narrative designed to fish for a few pats on the back.

Stein (2013) wrote that, "[w]hat millennials are most famous for besides narcissism is its effect: entitlement." My student's expectation that I'd be available, despite her not having kept in touch, to give up my planning time for her story and a few bucks for her cause highlights the "me, me, me" kind of selfish entitlement which typifies modern youth, right?

Not so fast. First, I love getting visits like these from former students even if they cost me my planning time. Part of the joy of teaching is being able to see students make strides in their personal and academic goals. It's true that they're not always polite or refined in asking for recommendations, donations, a listening ear, or for any of the other myriad needs of a secondary student, but the student–teacher dynamic is also not the same as a friendship between peers. Most teachers accept that there's going to be more giving than receiving in our profession, and part of being a good teacher is the expectation that students can visit with reasonable requests for support.

Don't get me wrong. I do think millennials are self-centered, but this issue is not entirely their fault, nor is it a trait specific to their generation more than it is their age. Biological and societal forces combine to make teens of all eras think of themselves before others.

Let's start with biology. Neuroscience educator Dee Coulter suggested that among the major periods of brain growth is one in the frontal lobes around the age of 15 and another in the same region around the age of 22. According to Coulter (2001), the frontal lobes are "marvelous organs for sensing patterns, having foresight, and for contributing a very vital skill: that of empathy and altruism." If we take into account variation in how quickly (or slowly) individuals mature, it's fair to say that teenagers from middle school to high school and even into college and beyond are still developing their biological capacity for seeing and understanding the world beyond themselves.

However, Goleman (1995) wrote, "[b]y late childhood the most advanced level of empathy emerges, as children are able to understand distress beyond the immediate situation, and to see that someone's condition or station in life may be a source of chronic distress" (p. 105). Examples of middle and high school students acting with and out of empathy throughout my career readily spring to mind. I remember a former student addressing the entire middle school on Veteran's Day and asking for clothing donations for wounded veterans, and I fondly recall the group of students who stepped up to form a student-run leadership/diversity committee in response to racial slurs being scrawled in our bathroom. In my current high school position, student efforts to help others range from asking for donations or selling products to actively volunteering time and energy to benefit a wide range of local charities, clubs, and organizations.

So, if middle school and high school students are capable of experiencing and demonstrating advanced levels of empathy, and brain biology is only partially responsible for their not doing so more often, why else are millennials so frequently seen as narcissistic?

Society bears part of the blame. First, there's the role of young people within society. Adolescents of all stages are considering some heavy questions, which basically emanate from the central one: "What's next for me?"

and spin off into more specific ones like, "Should I go to college? Will I be able to pay for college? Will I get a job and be able to support myself? Will I get married and have a family? Will I make an impact on the world? Will I be happy?"

Even if students don't ask these questions directly, it's easy to see how curiosity and uncertainty about the future unconsciously fuel the daily dramas that unfold each day in school hallways and reverberate through various social media channels. Students are trying to figure out how the world works and what it has in store for them. And, particularly in a day and age when spiraling college costs, mounting student loan debt, and even the debate over the relevance of college are topics of daily conversation, students feel backed into a corner. The inherent uncertainty of adolescence plus the added pressures of the modern economy promote a defensive "me-first" mentality.

As students ponder their futures, adults often add to the pressure. Parents, teachers, guidance counselors, and coaches ask, "What will you do next?" and remind students of the potential consequences of an unclear path. We push them to choose the right courses, do well on the right tests, sign up for more extra-curriculars, complete more service hours, and find part-time jobs to give them the best set of options for their future. Much of this guidance is a necessary part of being a parent or mentor, but we can't forget that we, as adults who have answered some of our own questions regarding family and career, are asking students to define their futures and state their identities as both continue to grow and develop.

From this vantage point, it's easy to see why kids are frequently accused and even guilty of narcissism. Adolescents who are still developing their biological capacity for empathy and altruism are asked by society to define their future and their identity before either of these has completely formed. We force students to focus on themselves, and then we often lament that they aren't more aware of and concerned about the issues of the world at large.

Though current economic concerns and the shifting landscape of higher education may be unique to millennials, adolescents of the past few generations have lived in a similar egocentric bubble. "[M]ost teens since post-World War II America . . . eagerly embraced opportunities to break away from their parents and establish their own cultural milieus, independence, and identities" (Watkins, 2009, p. 6). Perhaps the most notable feature that sets millennials apart is how public their lives are thanks to the advent and ubiquity of social media. Selfies and waves of self-indulgent

Tweets, Facebook statuses, Instagram posts, and the like certainly add to the narcissistic vibe of the millennial. But what if it's possible to use this self-centered perspective as a launch pad for better understanding of self and world?

Watkins (2009) wrote, "[a]s much as anything else, social and mobile media platforms enable young people to share stories about their day, their mood, and their lives through a wide array of digital content" and furthermore that, "[l]ife sharing, in the end, is as much about community as it is the individual" (p. 6). At first glance, adolescent social media posts may seem frivolous, but such posts are also casual attempts to connect. Students are identifying the parts of their days and themselves that they deem important, and they're offering them up for validation by their peers. What people of all ages fail to realize when posting to social media, however, is that we're not automatically or inherently interesting to others.

As Kleon (2012a) noted in *Steal Like an Artist*, "[t]he classroom is a wonderful, if artificial, place: Your professor gets paid to pay attention to your ideas, and your classmates are paying to pay attention to your ideas. Never again in your life will you have such a captive audience" (p. 77). If we really want others to connect with our stories and ideas, we need to be able to identify not only the ones that we want to share but also the ones that have value for an audience.

How do we take advantage of the simultaneous first-person focus along with the willingness and desire to share and at the same time foster reflection, understanding of self and world, and empathy for others? Furthermore, is it possible to do so while also addressing curricular goals and Common Core standards?

In *From Me to We: Using Narrative Nonfiction to Broaden Student Perspectives*, I present narrative nonfiction as a significant component to such learning. "Part I: Reading the Truth" focuses on developing a reading unit around a narrative nonfiction core text. "Part II: Writing the Truth" offers lessons and activities for students crafting their own personal essays or brief memoirs. While either Part could be used as a stand-alone unit, and activities and lessons from both Parts can be pulled to support existing units, the most powerful opportunity comes from the combination. Engaging with a grade-appropriate narrative nonfiction text followed by writing their own narrative nonfiction allows students to examine the world and the nature of truth through the lens of self, all while meeting a variety of reading, writing, and research standards.

By reading narrative nonfiction, students can explore much of the curricular plot and character content that they can through classic and contemporary fiction, but narrative nonfiction also offers a chance to experience vicarious perspectives from real lives. Gutkind (2012) wrote:

> experiencing the lives of other people, watching them in pain, indecision, and triumph, is incredibly rewarding and stimulating— and this intimate knowledge provides the opportunity to have a purpose in life, a goal beyond being a great writer. The creative nonfiction writer with a big issue or idea can wake up the world and make change happen. (p. 74)

Even psychology seems to have affirmed the power of literature to foster empathy and understanding of others. In an intriguing study, Castano and Kidd (2013) surmised from experiments with literary fiction that, "[f]iction seems also to expand our knowledge of others' lives, helping us recognize our similarity to them" (p. 377). While Castano and Kidd's experiments specifically centered on readers of fiction, it's hard to imagine that literary nonfiction does not offer similar benefits since, "[s]eeing things from another's perspective breaks down biased stereotypes, and so breeds tolerance and the acceptance of differences" (Goleman, 1995, p. 285). Reading the first-person perspective of others through narrative nonfiction allows us to walk in their shoes for a time and gain some understanding of their situation. The lessons from reading narrative nonfiction can be further enhanced by having students write their own.

At the 2014 *Creative Nonfiction* magazine conference in Pittsburgh, the writer Peter Trachtenberg suggested that the best narrative nonfiction starts with a question. As Lyons (2014) put it, "people are driven to create in order to understand something about themselves, the world, or their experiences and perceptions." If students can start with this perspective, then the first person becomes a vessel for exploration rather than just for gratuitous sharing.

Writing for discovery offers personal benefits, even if we don't share our work. Psychologist Timothy Wilson wrote in *Redirect: Changing the Stories We Live By* (2015) that, "[w]e usually don't have any trouble knowing how we feel, such as how happy, sad, angry, or elated we are at any given point in time. We are not very good, however, at knowing *why* we feel the way we do" (p. 27). Yet, it's important to examine the situations that generate our notable emotions because, "[t]he better we can understand and explain negative events such as relationship breakups, business failures, or medical problems, the faster we will recover from them" (Wilson, 2015, p. 54). Writing narrative nonfiction allows us to ponder the events in our lives in order to make meaning from them, and if we do so well enough and then choose to share our stories, our writing might even be useful to others.

Newkirk (2014) wrote:

> Events are not in our complete control, and humans face trauma and tragedy. Luck and chance play a huge role in any life. But even victims of terrible illness and loss are often able to derive meaning and benefit from their situation, perhaps working to inform or help others in their same situation. (p. 29)

Beyond personal benefit, if writers work to create what Gutkind (2012) called the ideal creative nonfiction piece, "a public subject with an intimate and personal spin" (p. 62), our work has a better chance of using the first-person perspective to connect with an audience.

I'm suggesting that, after students have been exposed to other first-person perspectives in quality narrative nonfiction mentor texts, teachers can empower students to embrace their self-centered adolescent nature in order to use it as a tool for self and world discovery. As Lopate (2013) wrote, "The solution to entrapment in the narcissistic hothouse of self is not to relinquish autobiographical writing, but to expand the self by bringing one's curiosity to interface with more and more history and the present world" (pp. 10–11).

Thus, through the effective pairing of reading and writing narrative nonfiction, millennials can be charged to modify a "this is me" perspective to that of "this is us." May the ideas and activities in this book help to inspire the shift.

Part

I

Reading the Truth

Chapter

Layers of Truth:
The Narrative Nonfiction Spiral

Student Snapshots

What can you get out of reading narrative nonfiction that you can't get out of other genres like fiction or poetry?

"Narrative nonfiction allows someone to experience real-life events that they would otherwise be ignorant of." Duncan C.

"Narrative nonfiction is factually relevant and still exciting. Pure fiction isn't true. Pure nonfiction is about as entertaining as a textbook. Narrative nonfiction is a good balance of the two." Sarah E.

What's one thing you learned from reading a narrative nonfiction book?

"It is very easy to point out society's faults, but it's very difficult to correct them." Sarah R.

"I learned that, where mental illness is concerned, treatment does not occur in a straight line. In some cases, one step forward was equivalent to two steps backward." Kara F.

"Mr. G, why can't we read something modern?" My tenth graders had just arrived back to the classroom from the library after picking up our class set of *A Separate Peace*, John Knowles's 1959 coming-of-age novel set during World War II, when one of my top-performing students let out a deep sigh and launched his question. Amid heads nodding in agreement and smirks of disgust from classmates who thumbed through the book's dusty pages, he continued.

"I mean, 1959? What does this have to do with me? You can't tell me there aren't more recent books that would be better for us to read." This particular student didn't usually interrupt class, so I listened patiently. Plus, he made a valid point.

After teaching eighth grade for 9 years, I made the bittersweet decision to move to a tenth grade position at the high school in my district. My decision was mostly logistical. I had just been hired as the head high school swim coach, my coaching schedule would line up better with the high school class schedule, and it made sense for me to be where my athletes were. However, I was also excited for a new grade level, a new challenge, and especially a fresh set of literature to explore with students. Upon looking at the school-board approved tenth grade reading list, however, it didn't take me long to notice two things: the entire list included only fiction, and most of it was pretty old. *A Separate Peace* provided the most current option for honors students while the regular college-bound sections could read Sandra Cisneros's *The House on Mango Street*, which had celebrated its twenty-fifth anniversary a few years before.

I do think reading classic fiction is valuable and important for students. My favorite book to read with students remains *To Kill a Mockingbird*, which I read with my eighth graders. Harper Lee's intricate plot, epic characters, and timeless lessons continue to resonate with readers today. I know many great teachers who do amazing things to help students connect to the magic of Shakespeare, for example, or to otherwise make classic texts relevant. That being said, I do wonder if secondary curricula that is dominated by classic fiction, as it was in my high school, is a disservice to students? Narrative nonfiction offers possibilities for lessons, activities, and learning that aren't as accessible through any other genre. It seemed clear that it was time to update our curricular reading list.

Furthermore, I wondered if we could kill two birds with one stone. Considering that our approved reading list was all fiction and all old, what if we added a contemporary nonfiction book? Doing so would not only diversify our stale curricular reading list, but it would also better align with the Common Core State Standards Initiative and, perhaps more importantly, align better with current trends in the modern literary landscape.

Thankfully, my department chair was receptive to taking new titles to be vetted by our school board and willing to scrounge into her budget to find money for copies of new books. Together, we brainstormed current possibilities for narrative nonfiction.

Creative, Literary, or Narrative? A Note on Nonfiction Terminology

Nonfiction storytelling has been saddled with many genre labels over the past few decades. Dinty Moore, editor of *Brevity*, a popular online journal devoted to flash nonfiction, lists creative nonfiction, literary nonfiction, narrative nonfiction, literature of fact, new journalism, and belles-lettres among these past genre labels (Moore, 2015, p. 9). In many cases, the three most currently popular labels of creative nonfiction, literary nonfiction, and narrative nonfiction are synonymous. All three "include memoir, literary journalism, the essay, and more . . ." (Moore, 2015, p. 9). Basically, the combination of literary or narrative techniques used to present lived experience, or simply plot plus truth, equals creative/narrative/literary nonfiction. So what's the difference between the terms?

Creative nonfiction seems to be the preferred term for creative writing journals and for creative writing MFA programs that offer a nonfiction concentration. The tagline of *Creative Nonfiction* magazine, one of the flagship journals of the genre, offers a succinct and pithy "true stories, well told" as both a tagline and a definition. The only problem with the modifier "creative" is that some authors feel it gives them permission to take liberties with the truth.

Take, for instance, the recent scandal surrounding Rachel Dolezal. When Dolezal, an NAACP chapter president in Spokane, was outed by her white parents for fabricating pieces of her own background, Dolezal claimed, in defense, to have engaged in creative nonfiction. Thomas Fate, a professor of creative writing, responded to the Dolezal scandal in a *Chicago Tribune* article.

Fate (2015) wrote:

Note that the "creative" in creative nonfiction doesn't allude to the freedom to fictionalize, but to use fictional craft strategies (for example, character development, dialogue, sensory detail) to write about true events. Sure, a memoirist or essayist constructs his own character and his own persona or voice. And yes, each writer's "truth" is subjective and interpreted and reliant on memory, but you can't invent new parents or conveniently omit key experiences that contradict your central point. (para. 3)

In other words, the "creative" in creative nonfiction may offer a cushion for the subjective nature of personal truth and for the fleeting nature of memory, but it doesn't allow for outright lies. Unfortunately, Dolezal is just the latest in a string of notorious writers and journalists to hide their fictions behind a label of "creative" truth. Previous offenders include James Frey (*A Million Little Pieces*), Brian Williams (NBC News), Stephen Glass (*The New Republic*), and Margaret B. Jones (*Love and Consequences: A Memoir of Hope and Survival*). Because of its ubiquity, I do teach my students the term creative nonfiction and where it applies, but because of the ambiguity of the modifier "creative," I don't use it as my primary instructional label.

The Common Core State Standards Initiative (which will be addressed more in Part II) uses the term literary nonfiction, which, as Moore (2015) pointed out, "has a nice ring to it but risks sounding a bit pretentious" (p. 7). I like "literary" better than "creative" as a modifier because it eliminates some ambiguity and offers broad possibilities for the genre, but I wonder if it might be too broad for students? The literary realm includes a vast scope of elements and qualities, and some are more appropriate to story-based nonfiction than others. If I introduce the term literary nonfiction to my students, they'll usually ask, "What's that?"

The term that my students have found to be the clearest, which requires the least explanation, and that avoids any ambiguity on their part is narrative nonfiction. When I ask my students if they enjoy reading nonfiction, they'll ask me what kind of nonfiction I mean. If I answer with narrative nonfiction as my chosen tag, they get it right away; "Oh, like autobiographies and stuff?"

The label of narrative nonfiction helps them instantly distinguish truth encapsulated in story from academic or news articles. Narrative nonfiction includes many of the sub-genres most frequently used in secondary ELA classes, including memoir, biography, literary journalism, and the personal essay, and it also is an effective term to talk about how to incorporate anecdotes into academic writing along with crafting hybrid forms like the college essay. Primarily because my students seem to resonate with the term the most, I've chosen narrative nonfiction as the core label in both my instruction and in this book, but, as with the genre at large, the terms literary nonfiction and creative nonfiction creep in and can mostly be considered synonyms.

Literary Nonfiction and the Common Core

As the Common Core State Standards (CCSS) Initiative continues to ripple across the educational landscape, a common reaction from teachers and various educational organizations is that there are both positive and negative aspects. There's a sort of, "it's a good start, but . . ." mentality surrounding many of the key features of the Common Core.

Certainly one of the more controversial aspects of the CCSS, from an English Language Arts teacher's perspective, is the call for students to engage with a greater percentage of informational texts than literary ones. Specifically, the "Key Design Consideration" section of the CCSS introduction on corestandards.org suggest that eighth graders should be reading a simple majority of informational texts (55 percent) to literary texts (45 percent) across their entire school curriculum. By twelfth grade, the suggested ratio grows to 70 percent informational texts and only 30 percent literary texts.

Some English Language Arts (ELA) teachers have protested this shift because they interpret it as a call to replace classic fiction, drama, and poetry with informational texts; however, a closer look at the Key Design Features section suggests that most of the strictly informational reading should be done in subjects (like history, science, math, etc.) outside of the ELA classroom. Furthermore, the CCSS acknowledges the complicated role of the modern ELA teacher, which includes continuing to teach fiction, drama, poetry, and other literary texts along with paying "greater attention to a specific category of informational text—literary nonfiction—than has been traditional."

Placing literary nonfiction standards in the category of informational text highlights both the range and versatility of the genre as well as the problematic nature of the label itself. Literary nonfiction has both literary (plot, setting, characters, theme, tone, etc.) and informational (author's purpose, examining claims, fact vs. opinion, etc.) elements and can, therefore, simultaneously satisfy different aspects from both categories. Furthermore, a well-designed narrative nonfiction unit, which includes both reading and writing components, allows students to engage not only with the informational and literary aspects of the literacy standards but also research and writing standards as well (Appendix C includes a list of Common Core standards satisfied by corresponding activities presented in this book). So, I'd argue that the highlighting of literary nonfiction as a significant area of focus is definitely a positive aspect of the CCSS Initiative, but it also exposes a key negative, which is the potentially unnecessary separation of overlapping categories of standards.

As Newkirk (2014) noted, "We are biologically predisposed to process experience though the lens of antecedents and consequences" (p. 24), and we thereby apply a sense of plot to texts like graduation speeches, political candidates' stories, scientific theories, etc. Even texts, like academic or news articles, which can be more purely labelled as informational, overlap some with literary texts. "As readers, we are never face-to-face with raw reality, whatever that might look like. Information of almost any kind comes to us through some teller, some guide, and some authorial presence" (Newkirk, 2014, p. 69). Whether the author is identified and present as a first-person narrator in the story, or hidden behind the objective third-person, there is still an author behind the scene making rhetorical choices about content and sequence.

Recognizing an authorial presence is important in all types of texts because "[n]o longer are we merely holding opinions different from one another; we're also holding different facts" (Manjoo, 2008, p. 2). In a day and age of increasingly polarized news outlets and even research institutions, readers must be able to understand an author's context to fully understand the information or argument presented. We live in an era where it's easy for an author to "go about the business of persuasion covertly, without divulging their motives or even the fact that they're engaged in persuasion" (Manjoo, 2008, p. 192). More than ever, literary narrative is a vessel for delivering information or for encapsulating argument.

While the blending of the narrative, informative, and persuasive modes does call for teaching more critical awareness to young readers, the blurred boundaries are not necessarily a bad thing. Lee Gutkind noted in his keynote presentation at the 2014 *Creative Nonfiction* magazine conference in Pittsburgh that "Readers remember more facts for a longer period of time when communicated with story. Stories with people and action help [a writer to] 'sneak in or embed' information and facts." Nowhere is this pattern of information embedded in story (often to make an argument) better exhibited than through the format of TED talks, a type of text that's gaining popularity and ubiquity for use in academic classes of all disciplines.

In a way, it could be argued that narrative nonfiction texts are a more honest means of delivering information and making an argument, because, rather than the author's background and story being hidden behind the objective third-person, the narrative provides context. We can see, through the story, why the author includes the facts and makes the arguments that he or she does.

The CCSS Initiative is on point by highlighting the importance of literary nonfiction in secondary ELA curricula, but this importance doubles when considering the variety of popular ways that nonfiction is consumed in the world beyond the classroom.

Narrative Nonfiction and the Modern Literary Landscape

An even more significant cause than the Common Core for including narrative nonfiction as a key component in secondary ELA curricula is the state of the modern literary landscape.

Besides being a popular kind of narrative nonfiction in its own right, the most popular TED talks have been developed into full-length books. Sir Ken Robinson's TED talk "Do Schools Kill Creativity?" (Robinson, 2006) became the book *The Element: How Finding Your Passion Changes Everything* (Robinson & Aronica, 2009). Brené Brown's TED talk "The Power of Vulnerability" (Brown, 2010) became *Daring Greatly: How the Courage to be Vulnerable Changes the Way We Live* (Brown, 2012). Susan Cain's "The Power of Introverts" became *Quiet: The Power of Introverts in a World that Can't Stop Talking* (Cain, 2012). Austin Kleon adapted "Steal like an Artist" on TED (Kleon, 2012b) into *Steal like an Artist: 10 Things Nobody Told You about Being Creative* (Kleon, 2012a). Not only have many of these authors written sequels, but their books blend information and argument into their narratives, just like the TED format.

The modern literary landscape also includes some notable examples of nonfiction narratives influencing events in the real world. In 2014, Malala Yousafzai was awarded the Nobel Peace Prize, thanks, in part, to the popularity of her memoir *I Am Malala: The Girl Who Stood Up for Education and was Shot by the Taliban* (Yousafzai & Lamb, 2013). While inspirational under any circumstances, it's interesting to consider whether Malala's narrative would have had the far-reaching impact it did without the vessel of a best-selling memoir.

Also in 2014, the narrative nonfiction podcast *Serial* (a spin-off of *This American Life*, another popular narrative nonfiction podcast) went viral. Not only was the first season of *Serial* awarded a Peabody in 2015 and renewed for two forthcoming seasons, but the series cast enough doubt on the 2000 conviction of Adnan Syed in the murder of his ex-girlfriend Hae Min Lee that early steps towards a fresh appeal by Syed's legal team have been successful (The Guardian, 2016).

The modern literary landscape includes an incredible overlap of pop-culture, new and old media and mediums, and real events. Books, films, blogs, podcasts, YouTube clips, TED talks, and more mesh together, complement, and inform one another, and the main roads of intersection are story and truth: narrative nonfiction.

The modern literary landscape is one where Allie Brosch can write and illustrate her comical graphic memoir *Hyperbole and a Half* (Brosch, 2013) (based on her blog, http://hyperboleandahalf.blogspot.co.uk), and then appear as a guest on comedian Marc Maron's popular *WTF* podcast (www.wtfpod.com) where the two swapped stories of the kinds of depression that haunts them both (and becomes fodder for their creative work). Mendelsohn (2010) wrote, "This experience of being constantly exposed to other people's life stories is matched only by the inexhaustible eagerness of people to tell their life stories."

Perhaps the most plentiful examples of the pervasiveness of narrative nonfiction can be found at the movie theater, where new Hollywood adaptations of popular memoirs and works of literary journalism seem to debut weekly. As 2014 rolled over into 2015, five films based on popular narrative nonfiction books were in theaters at the same time. These films included *Unbroken* (based on Laura Hillenbrand's book of the same name), *Wild* (based on Cheryl Strayed's memoir of the same name), *The Theory of Everything* (based on Jane Wilde Hawking's memoir *Travelling to Infinity: My Life with Stephen*); *The Imitation Game* (based on Andrew Hodges's biography *Alan Turing: The Enigma*); and *American Sniper* (based on Chris Kyle's autobiography of the same name).

Big-name Hollywood stars lead the charge to bring these true stories to the silver screen. Clint Eastwood directed *American Sniper* with Bradley Cooper starring as Chris Kyle. Reese Witherspoon reportedly bought the film rights to Strayed's *Wild* before the memoir was even published. Robert Redford and Nick Nolte starred as the main characters in the film adaptation of Bill Bryson's epic Appalachian Trail memoir *A Walk in the Woods* (with Redford also directing). A film version of the Christopher

McDougall's *Born to Run: A Hidden Tribe, Superathletes, and the Greatest Race the World has Never Seen* (the book that inspired booms in barefoot running and minimal running shoe technology) has been announced with Matthew McConaughey set to play Caballo Blanco, one of the book's central characters.

Often, the process of adapting nonfiction books into "based-on-a-true-story" films comes with interesting true behind-the-scenes stories in addition. While directing *Unbroken*, Angelina Jolie struck up a friendship with an elderly Louie Zamperini, whose younger self was the central character of both the book and the film. Shortly before Zamperini's death, Jolie gave him an early screening of the film. Jane Wilde Hawking wrote an earlier, much more bitter and critical version of her memoir detailing her life with Stephen Hawking. After she and Stephen reconciled, she revised her memoir, which was the version that was adapted into *The Theory of Everything*. The film *Steve Jobs*, starring Michael Fassbender in the titular role, is the sanctioned film version of Walter Isaacson's biography (which the real Jobs commissioned), while the filmmakers of the 2013 film *Jobs*, starring Ashton Kutcher, received no help or sanctioning from the actual people featured in Jobs' narrative (some of whom were involved in starting to make the latter film).

Because of both the ubiquity and popularity of narrative nonfiction in the tandem form of print and film, and also because of the interesting behind-the-scenes stories and easy forays into related works of nonfiction, the pairing of a narrative nonfiction text and a corresponding film version is at the heart of a valuable kind of text set for secondary students.

The Narrative Nonfiction Spiral

As I searched for viable contemporary nonfiction to add to our tenth grade reading list, I first noticed the frequent memoir to movie pattern (Figure 1.1 comprises a list of notable nonfiction book/film pairings), but when I got to John Krakauer's tandem survival narratives *Into Thin Air* and *Into the Wild*, I also noticed a sub-pattern. A number of popular memoir/movie combos started first as articles in journalistic publications (Figure 1.2 comprises a list of nonfiction articles adapted into books adapted into films). Krakauer published versions of both *Into the Wild* and *Into Thin Air* in *Outside* magazine before he published them as books and then they were made into films (*Into Thin Air* actually had two film versions: a made for TV version in the 1990s and then the recent big budget blockbuster *Everest*).

Figure 1.1 Notable Narrative Nonfiction Books that were Adapted into Films (Arranged Alphabetically by Book Title)

Book	Author	Film
The Accidental Billionaires: The Founding of Facebook: A Tale of Sex, Money, Genius, and Betrayal	Ben Mezrich	*The Social Network* (2010)
Alan Turing: The Enigma	Andrew Hodges	*The Imitation Game* (2014)
Alive	Piers Paul Read	*Alive* (1993)
Angela's Ashes	Frank McCourt	*Angela's Ashes* (1999)
The Astronaut Wives Club: A True Story	Lily Koppel	*The Astronaut Wives Club* (ABC TV Series 2015–)
The Autobiography of Malcolm X	(as told to) Alex Haley	*Malcolm X* (1992)
The Basketball Diaries	Jim Carroll	*The Basketball Diaries* (1995)
A Beautiful Mind: The Life of Mathematical Genius and Nobel Laureate John Nash	Sylvia Nasar	*A Beautiful Mind* (2001)
The Big Short: Inside the Doomsday Machine	Michael Lewis	*The Big Short* (2015)
Big Sur	Jack Kerouac	*Big Sur* (2013)
Born to Run: A Hidden Tribe, Superathletes, and the Greatest Race the World has Never Seen	Christopher McDougall	*Born to Run* (2016)
Bury my Heart at Wounded Knee: An Indian History of the American West	Dee Brown	*Bury My Heart at Wounded Knee* (HBO Film 2007)
Dead Man Walking: An Eyewitness Account of the Death Penalty in the United States	Sister Helen Prejean	*Dead Man Walking* (1995)
The Finest Hours: The True Story of the U.S. Coast Guard's Most Daring Sea Rescue	Michael J. Tougias and Casey Sherman	*The Finest Hours* (2016)
The Freedom Writers Diary: How a Teacher and 150 Teens Used Writing to Change Themselves and the World Around Them	The Freedom Writers with Erin Gruwell	*Freedom Writers* (2007)
Friday Night Lights: A Town, a Team, and a Dream	Buzz Bissinger	*Friday Night Lights* (2004) *Friday Night Lights* (NBC TV Series 2006–2011)
Gandhi: His Life and Message for the World	Louis Fischer	*Gandhi* (1980)
In the Heart of the Sea: The Tragedy of the Whaleship Essex	Nathaniel Philbrick	*In the Heart of the Sea* (2015)
Jarhead: A Marine's Chronicle of the Gulf War and Other Battles	Anthony Swofford	*Jarhead* (2005)
Long Walk to Freedom	Nelson Mandela	*Long Walk to Freedom* (2013)
Marley and Me: Life and Love with the World's Worst Dog	John Grogan	*Marley and Me* (2008)
The Monuments Men: Allied Heroes, Nazi Thieves, and the Greatest Treasure Hunt in History	Robert M. Edsel and Bret Witter	*The Monuments Men* (2014)

Book	Author	Film
My Week with Marilyn	Colin Clark	*My Week with Marilyn* (2011)
On the Road	Jack Kerouac	*On the Road* (2012)
Orange is the New Black: My Year in a Women's Prison	Piper Kerman	*Orange is the New Black* (Netflix TV series 2013–)
The Perfect Storm: A True Story of Men Against the Sea	Sebastian Junger	*The Perfect Storm* (2000)
The Pianist: The Extraordinary True Story of One Man's Survival: 1939–1945	Wladyslaw Szpilman	*The Pianist* (2002)
Playing the Enemy: Nelson Mandela and the Game that Made a Nation	John Carlin	*Invictus* (2009)
The Right Stuff	Tom Wolfe	*The Right Stuff* (1983)
A River Runs Through It and Other Stories	Norman Maclean	*A River Runs Through It* (1992)
The Rum Diary	Hunter S. Thompson	*The Rum Diary* (2011)
Seven Years in Tibet: My Life Before, During, and After	Heinrich Harrar	*Seven Years in Tibet* (1997)
Steve Jobs	Walter Isaacson	*Steve Jobs* (2015)
The Taliban Shuffle: Strange Days in Afghanistan and Pakistan	Kim Barker	*Whiskey, Tango, Foxtrot (The Taliban Shuffle)* (2016)
Team of Rivals: The Political Genius of Abraham Lincoln	Doris Kearns Goodwin	*Lincoln* (2012)
To Reach the Clouds: My High Wire Walk Between the Twin Towers	Phillipe Petit	*The Walk* (2015)
Travelling to Infinity: My Life with Stephen	Jane Wilde Hawking	*The Theory of Everything* (2014)
True Story: Murder, Memoir, Mea Culpa	Michael Finkel	*True Story* (2015)
Twelve Years a Slave	Solomon Northup	*12 Years a Slave* (2013)
Unbroken: A World War II Story of Survival, Resilience, and Redemption	Laura Hillenbrand	*Unbroken* (2014)
Under the Tuscan Sun: At Home in Italy	Frances Mayes	*Under the Tuscan Sun* (2003)
A Walk in the Woods: Rediscovering America on the Appalachian Trail	Bill Bryson	*A Walk in the Woods (2015)*
We Bought a Zoo: The Amazing True Story of a Young Family, a Broken Down Zoo, and the 200 Wild Animals that Changed their Lives Forever	Benjamin Mee	*We Bought a Zoo* (2011)
Wild: From Lost to Found on the Pacific Crest Trail	Cheryl Strayed	*Wild* (2014)
The Wolf of Wall Street	Jordan Belfort	*The Wolf of Wall Street* (2013)

Figure 1.2 Notable Articles that Became Books that were Adapted into Films (Arranged Alphabetically by Book Title)

Article	Book	Author	Film
"Black Hawk Down: An American War Story," The *Philadelphia Inquirer* Article Series	*Black Hawk Down: A Story of Modern War*	Mark Bowden	*Blackhawk Down* (2001)
"The Ballad of Big Mike," *The New York Times*	*The Blind Side: Evolution of a Game*	Michael Lewis	*The Blind Side* (2009)
"Bennet Omalu, Concussions, and the NFL: How One Doctor Changed Football Forever," *GQ Magazine*	No book adaptation	Jeanne Marie Laskas	*Concussion* (2015)
"Fast-Food Nation" Article Series, *Rolling Stone*	*Fast-Food Nation: The Dark Side of the All-American Meal*	Eric Schlosser	*Fast-Food Nation* (2006)
"The Killer Elite," *Rolling Stone*	*Generation Kill: Devil Dogs, Iceman, Captain America, and the New Face of American War*	Evan Wright	*Generation Kill* (HBO Mini-series, 2008)
"In Cold Blood," Article Series, *The New Yorker*	*In Cold Blood*	Truman Capote	*In Cold Blood* (1967)
"Death of an Innocent," *Outside*	*Into the Wild*	Jon Krakauer	*Into the Wild* (2007)
"Into Thin Air," *Outside*	*Into Thin Air*	Jon Krakauer	*Into Thin Air* (1997 TV Movie) *Everest* (2015)
"The Trading Desk," *The New York Times Magazine*	*Moneyball: The Art of Winning an Unfair Game*	Michael Lewis	*Moneyball* (2011)
"The Great Escape: How the CIA Used a Fake Sci-Fi Flick to Rescue Americans from Tehran," *Wired*	*The Master of Disguise: My Secret Life in the CIA*	Joshuah Bearman (Article) Tony Mendez (Book)	*Argo* (2012)
"Four Good Legs Between Us," *American Heritage*	*Seabiscuit: An American Legend*	Laura Hillenbrand	*Seabiscuit* (2003)
"He Has the World on Two Strings," *The Los Angeles Times*	*The Soloist: A Lost Dream, and Unlikely Friendship, and the Redemptive Power of Music*	Steve Lopez	*The Soloist* (2009)

In the overarching story, the article spirals into the book, which spirals into the film, and each text adds a new layer. The article lays the foundation by introducing the characters, plot, and premise; the book extends or deepens the elements introduced in the article to tell a longer or more complete story, and the film condenses true events and often adds fictional elements to conform to Hollywood standards and/or appeal to a mass market audience. Any of these texts are gateways or entry points into the larger story. Watching the movie might lead to reading the book, which a reader may then compare with the original article, or any combination of one related text leading to the next.

For example, after watching the first season of *Orange is the New Black* on Netflix, I picked up Piper Kerman's memoir of the same name on which the series was based (Kerman, 2010). As I suspected, the series was highly fictionalized, though it was interesting to note how certain threads that Kerman introduced in the book were explored and incorporated into the series. The memoir raised important questions about iniquities in the modern prison system, and I might never have picked up the book had I not first watched the series.

Similarly, a positive magazine review led me to watch the HBO miniseries *Generation Kill*, which was based on embedded *Rolling Stone* journalist Evan Wright's account of his time with the 1st Reconnaissance Marine Battalion during Operation Iraqi Freedom in 2003 (Wright, 2004). After watching the series, I picked up Wright's memoir (an extension of the article he first wrote for *Rolling Stone*). Expecting the memoir to expose similar levels of fictionalization in the television adaptation as I had experienced with *Orange is the New Black*, I was surprised to discover that HBO was extremely faithful to Wright's narrative.

Considering that my gateway into the *Generation Kill* text set was a magazine review, there's another aspect of the story spiral: supporting and ancillary nonfiction. When a popular memoir or piece of literary journalism is published, it's often followed by a series of book reviews and interviews with the author and sometimes even with the real-life subjects and characters. Readers search for resources connected to the books they enjoy. These may include news articles about the events included in the book, Google Image searches for pictures of authors and real-life characters, YouTube video searches for interviews and related content, and/or informational searches to help fill in background knowledge related to the book.

Figure 1.3 The Narrative Nonfiction Spiral

The Narrative Nonfiction Spiral

Literary Journalism
Magazine or Newspaper
Feature Story

NEWS

Narrative Nonfiction Novel

Supporting Nonfiction:
• Book Reviews
• Interviews with author and real-life subjects/characters about book
• Articles and videos about content and ideas raised in story

Supporting Nonfiction:
• Movie Reviews
• Interviews with film director and cast about story
• Interviews with author and real-life subjects/characters about film
• "Making of" documentaries

Based on a True Story (BOTS) Film

Each medium spirals into the next, adding a new layer and perspective to the story. Each layer also offers different gateways into the story for readers/viewers.

When a narrative nonfiction book is adapted into a film, a new round of supporting nonfiction fires up. There are movie reviews, interviews with the director and film cast on how they feel about the book, interviews with the author and real-life characters on how they feel about the film, behind the scenes "making-of" documentaries, etc. These short and easily accessible works of supporting nonfiction can also provide a gateway into the text set; a review or interview may lead a reader/viewer to watch the film or read the book (as did the review of *Generation Kill* in my case). So, as articles spiral into books, which spiral into movies, there are also supporting works of nonfiction that spiral off each of these core texts and transitions. Figure 1.3 is a visual representation of this narrative nonfiction spiral.

Not only does the narrative nonfiction spiral represent the ways in which a real-world reader/viewer may approach related texts of a story, it also provides a pattern for a rich and interesting text set for a secondary literature unit. A narrative nonfiction article can serve as pre-reading for students to begin to build background knowledge and generate questions about both the story's plot and its key content. Those questions segue nicely into reading the narrative nonfiction book as the unit's core text, with whole-class discussion activities and exploring supporting nonfiction to socially construct meaning. Finally, watching the film version allows students to compare and contrast the book's account with Hollywood's version. Not only can students analyze the filmmaker's choices, but they can also discuss whether or not those choices were effective.

After considering a number of choices, my department chair and I settled on Steve Lopez's (2008) *The Soloist: A Lost Dream, and Unlikely Friendship, and Redemptive Power of Music* as our choice for a fresh addition to our tenth grade curriculum, and our school board approved it. Lopez, a journalist for the *Los Angeles Times*, started writing the story about his friendship with Nathaniel Anthony Ayers, a talented musician who suffers from schizophrenia that contributed to his homelessness, as part of his weekly newspaper column. The popular column was adapted into the book (part memoir, part literary journalism), and the book was adapted into a Hollywood film starring Robert Downey, Jr. and Jamie Foxx as Lopez and Ayers, respectively.

Chapter 2 of this book will outline a sequence of activities for which a teacher could select a text set from Figure 1.1 or 1.2 (or a similar text set) and design an engaging narrative nonfiction unit. Chapter 3 will include the same sequence of activities specific to Lopez's *The Soloist* along with sample work from my students.

Chapter

2

Exploring the Truth: Activities for Reading Narrative Nonfiction

Student Snapshots

What can you get out of reading narrative nonfiction that you can't get out of other genres like fiction or poetry?

"You get a sense of real life problems in real time." Tanna H.

"Knowing that a story actually happened tends to bring the reader a little closer to what they are reading." Sam B.

What's one thing you learned from reading a narrative nonfiction book?

"Nonfiction can be more than a textbook or a biography, but a story with an actual plot." Bryce D.

"Every single person has a background and a life that means something." Mackenzie J.

"Mr. G, why can't we pick our own books to read?" This is another common question students have asked when I've announced the anchor text of a curricular reading unit, and it's a fair one that applies to English teachers too, regarding books that we teach.

Truth be told, I don't love every book that I've had to teach. Sometimes our curricular novels are not the ones teachers would personally choose, but logistics including the cost of new books, the administrative approval process, and overlap with other grade levels' reading lists prevent us from adopting our preferred books. In some cases, such lack of preference is part of the job, and, like other English teachers, I can find literary, cultural, and canonical value even in books that I don't personally enjoy. Being able to appreciate elements of things you don't enjoy is not a bad critical skill to teach to students.

However, it's hard to sell a book you're not passionate about, especially when you know there are potentially more engaging ones out there that demonstrate similar themes and literary elements and would empower similar (or better) conversations among contemporary students. Kelly Gallagher (2009) suggested, "If we want our students to do a lot more reading than they are currently doing, they need to be immersed in a pool of high-interest reading material" (p. 30). The key to any successful reading unit is student engagement, and in order to most effectively engage students, a teacher ideally has a personal love of the book in question to help energize instruction. Certainly one way to maximize personal connection to reading instruction is to let students individually choose their own books. A number of recent research and commentary pieces highlight the benefits of student choice with regards to reading.

I believe there should be a significant place for student choice and independent reading in secondary ELA curriculum, but I also agree with Gallagher (2009), who wrote "[T]here is a real value that can only be found when the entire class is reading the same title" (p. 91). Such value largely comes through class discussion. Ulin (2010) noted that when we read and respond, "[W]e join a broader conversation, by which we both transcend ourselves and are enlarged" (p. 151). The type of conversation that Ulin describes sounds quite like Rosenblatt's (1978) Transactional Theory of Reader Response where the interaction between reader and text generates meaning. And, our individual conversations with texts can be further enhanced by group discussion. "The group is less likely than the individual to miss something. Conversation yields more robust understanding for all" (Hammond & Nessel, 2011, p. 88). When students help each other through discussion and activity, it takes reading and responding from individual acts into social construction of knowledge.

As an English teacher, I see myself as an ambassador for books that I love. As Dorfman and Capelli (2007) recognized, "The first criterion [for choosing a mentor text] is that [the teacher] must connect with the book and love it" (p. 4). If I skillfully share what I love and appreciate about a given book, I can open a pathway to similar appreciation among my students. But, it's not enough for me to passively express the value I find in a book. Because I recognize that different readers have different tastes, I don't get mad or take it personally if my students don't love the same books that I do, but if, rather than simply labeling a book as great, I design activities to help students discover a book's value for themselves, I improve my chances of helping to engage more readers. "[V]aluable classroom time presents the best opportunity—often the only opportunity—to turn kids onto reading" (Gallagher, 2009, p. 2).

It's with these principles in mind that I present an outline for a narrative nonfiction reading unit following the spiral pattern I presented in Chapter 1. While many of these activities could likely be applied with success to an independent choice reading unit, I present them as a whole-class reading unit centered on class discussion of the themes and elements of the selected anchor text and of the larger narrative nonfiction genre as a whole. Through this approach, I hope to transfer my passion for this genre, and even if my students don't love my anchor text selection, they can develop an understanding of the elements and an appreciation for the greater value of the genre (as I'll demonstrate further in Chapter 3).

The challenge of setting up a reading unit based on a narrative nonfiction anchor text is to tap into the same energy that high-interest fiction provides while also highlighting unique aspects of the genre. Ulin (2010) wrote that, "[B]ooks enlarge us by giving us direct access to experiences not our own" (p. 16), and I find this holds particularly true with narrative nonfiction. The benefit of the narrative nonfiction spiral is that it sets up a natural unit sequence to promote student discussion and engagement. By selecting a text set following the pattern shown in Figure 1.2 (a literary journalism article being adapted into a book, which is then adapted into a film), a pre-reading, anchor text, and post-reading sequence easily emerges for arranging a curricular reading unit. Figure 2.1 presents a visual arrangement of this sequence along with corresponding activities, which are explained in greater detail in this chapter.

Figure 2.1 The Narrative Nonfiction Spiral Progression

The Narrative Nonfiction Spiral Progression

Teacher Activities

- Set up a reading calendar
- Curate supporting nonfiction materials
- Collect and organize students' pre-reading questions into a class list

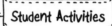

Student Activities

Pre-Reading
Literary Journalism Article

- Read article
- Make a list of pre-reading inquiry questions– what do you want to know more about?

- Set up a Google Doc to share with classes for collaborative chapter notes
- Schedule activities with supporting nonfiction at appropriate times in the reading calendar
- Coordinate discussion throughout
- Make a list of topics for the I-I-I Research Paper

Anchor Text
Narrative Nonfiction Novel

- Read Novel
- Complete regular chapter assessments
- Contribute to collaborative chapter notes
- Complete "empathy check-ins"– How do you feel about narrator/characters, and why?
- Watch, read, discuss, and write about supporting nonfiction
- Complete the I-I-I Research Paper

Optional:
Contact the author, a real-life character from the story, or a subject expert for a classroom visit or Skype Q+A

Post-Reading
Film Adaptation of Novel

- Watch Film
- Compare and contrast film version with book
- Evaluate: why did filmmakers change what they did? Was it effective?

Culminating Assessment
Write a Personal Essay

1. Pre-Reading: Literary Journalism Article

Frontloading, or providing contextual information for an anchor text before students read it, is a popular method for introducing a reading unit. The danger of excessive frontloading, however, is that it can emotionally dampen the reading experience if there's nothing left for students to discover. In order to promote a spirit of reading for discovery, I find it's better to start with questions rather than answers.

Beginning with an article or relatively short journalistic piece as an entry point into the larger text set provides a basis for student inquiry. Using the article as a launch pad, students can generate a variety of questions including plot-based questions (Why did "x" happen? What happens next? Will "y" happen?), questions about the content (ideas, issues, allusions, and/or vocabulary presented in the article), and broader "big questions" (How does this article relate to me? What does this article suggest about society? What are the important topics for us to discuss in response to this article?).

If you are using an anchor text from Figure 1.1, or a narrative nonfiction book that has been adapted into a film with no preceding article, you can substitute a supplementary article for this pre-reading step. Consider a book review; a film review; an interview with the author, film director, or one of the real-life characters featured in the story; or a news article highlighting some of the plot points from the story—any article that provides just a taste of the story's plot and some relevant background information should do the trick. The goal is to get students engaged in and asking questions about the story, the story's content, and the broader genre.

Student Activities during Pre-Reading

◆ Read the article. Annotate it in any way you'd like in order to identify interesting parts, record questions, or label places you'd like to discuss further.

◆ Make a list of five questions. What do you want to know more about? What are you curious about and hope is addressed or answered in the novel?

Teacher Preparation during Pre-Reading

◆ Set up a reading calendar for the anchor text and the major unit activities. Consider how long you can devote to the unit, and plug in any school events, holidays, or schedule interruptions. Then, try to balance a moderate nightly pace that keeps quick readers from getting bored and doesn't stress slower readers too much. Because I know that some discussions will take more time than others and students will be more enthusiastic about some chapters and activities than others, I like to build in periodic "catch-up days" with no reading homework so we can tie up loose ends between sections of the anchor text.

◆ Curate supporting nonfiction texts. What articles, videos, essays, songs, photographs, etc., are important to this story and text set and will help students engage with the story or its broader content and questions? Start to gather these ancillary sources, and bookmark places in the core text and reading calendar where students will most benefit from engaging with these supporting texts.

◆ Organize and categorize students' pre-reading questions into a class list. Combine similar questions, eliminate frivolous ones, and arrange 15–25 of the most common/relevant pre-reading questions into thematic categories to redistribute to the class. This collective list can serve as a reading guide with periodic check-ins during the reading of the anchor text to see which have been answered so far.

Reading the article, generating personal questions and considering the questions of classmates, and engaging in a preliminary discussion around these activities help student readers to feel invested. It's natural to want to read on to find out what happens and to discover the answers to our questions.

2. Anchor Text: Narrative Nonfiction Novel

Once students have read the pre-reading article and generated their questions, it's time to get them into the novel without further ado. I prefer to let students first read without encumbering them with annotations or other immediate tasks that pull them out of the story. Granted, assigned reading is somewhat artificial when compared with self-selected reading for pleasure, but most of us don't stop to take notes the first time we read something just as "we don't ask students to stop the films they watch every five minutes so they can discuss foreshadowing, developing themes, and the director's tone" (Gallagher, 2009, p. 61), and I think the same should apply to assigned reading in English class.

Annotating is a wonderful tool for digging back into the book for textual evidence on a second or third read or skim through, but "[t]oo many notes can get overwhelming, interposing the reader's sensibility on the writer's until the latter is obscured" (Ulin, 2010, p. 49).

Hammond and Nessel (2011) wrote:

> Reading and discussing should occupy the large majority of class-room time because this is what students must learn to do well . . . their abilities to make inferences, draw conclusions, follow sequences, note cause–effect relationships, discern main ideas, and so on are readily evident when the teacher engages them in sub-stantive discussions about texts. (p. 54)

In order to avoid students "drowning in marginalia and a sea of sticky notes" (Gallagher, 2009, p. 5), I recommend a simple and effective sequence of activities for the anchor text, based primarily on reading and discussion.

Student Activities while Reading the Anchor Text

Regular Chapter Assessments
I prefer low-risk daily reading quizzes to assess and encourage student reading. I mostly give short (five questions or so) chapter quizzes consisting of multiple choice, true/false, and short answer questions based on major plot points, but I mix it up sometimes by having students write a one-paragraph summary of the chapter, or having students write their own quiz questions based on the chapter. While these daily assessments do provide a mechanism for students to earn a small recurring grade, and thereby promote student investment, they also serve a larger purpose. When we review the answers, I direct students to the appropriate passages in the text, and the textual evidence springboards us into deeper discussion. The quiz allows for a brief chapter review, and then we use that recall as a basis to discuss the significance of the key events along with the bigger questions.

Collaborative Chapter Notes
Using my last name to play off of the once popular Cliff Notes study guides, I used to give my students handouts that I called Griff Notes. I'd use Griff Notes as a way to help students organize major pieces of our

discussion including plot-based questions and themes along with literary elements and vocabulary. Students would work individually, in pairs, or in small groups to consider the questions and the context of the vocabulary, and then we'd share out and discuss as a class.

Building on this simple and successful technique, I recently started using collaborative platforms like Google Docs so that student groups can actually co-create our chapter notes rather than me providing them. Small groups of students can each select or be assigned a chapter from the anchor text to review and discuss and, through the collaborative chapter notes, they contribute to a document that the rest of the class can access and benefit from. Figure 2.2 shows a basic collaborative chapter notes template that students can contribute to via Google Docs.

The components of the collaborative chapter notes can be customized to include categories that are specific to the anchor text, the teacher's preferences, or the students' needs, but effective basic components include vocabulary, allusions, and plot-based discussion questions.

- *Vocabulary*: Of course it's important for teachers to identify and curate essential vocabulary terms from the chapters, but the benefit of the collaborative note activity is that students can also curate terms. Especially in narrative nonfiction, sometimes it's hard to know what content and context specific words students might be unfamiliar with.
- *Allusions*: I call this category our "to-Google" list. Allusions are an important component to studying narrative nonfiction because true stories often reference real politicians and celebrities, places, historical events, and cultural references that students are unfamiliar with. I've heard many teachers lament about students "leaving our schools without the cultural literacy needed to be productive citizens in a democratic society" (Gallagher, 2009, p. 30).

Figure 2.2 Collaborative Chapter Notes Template

Chapter	Vocabulary	Allusions (To Google)	Plot-based Discussion Questions
1			
2			
3			

By examining the allusions within a narrative nonfiction novel, students can learn a lot about the intertwining facets of the real world, and the narrative framework helps them contextualize, understand, and remember this learning.

◆ *Plot-based discussion points and questions*: Hammond and Nessel (2011) noted that "the teacher's words and actions are critical to initiating and sustaining the discussion and to helping the students see themselves as capable, thinking readers" (p. 42). Once teachers have demonstrated important plot-based discussion points and questions from the early chapters, students have a model for identifying their own in later chapters. What are the big events, topics, and broader questions from this chapter? Once student groups list those items in this column, the rest of the class has a guide for further discussion.

Empathy Check-Ins

One of the other unique aspects of the narrative nonfiction genre is that the author is presenting real-life people as characters (including him or herself, if it's a memoir). It's important to remind students of the constant "authorial presence" (Newkirk, 2014, p. 69) that's guiding and constructing the character portrayals, and to ask students to evaluate the impact of these perspectives on the narrative and our reactions to it. Since personal narratives are an effective component in emotional appeals, I like to ask students to zoom out from the text to analyze how author portrayals of characters can affect readers' reactions.

By continuously asking questions like:

◆ Do you like the narrator? Why or why not?
◆ Is the narrator fair? Why or why not?
◆ Regardless of whether you like the narrator, do you trust him/her? Why or why not?
◆ What do you think of [character x]? Do you care what happens to him/her? Why or why not?

. . . we encourage students to examine how the narrative presentation and the portrayal of characters has affected them. The first question identifies the emotional reaction, and the follow-up asks students to link that reaction to specific textual evidence. I call this line of questioning an "empathy check-in."

Supporting Nonfiction

Gallagher (2009) wrote, "It is imperative that we augment every novel our students read with real-world texts that shows them that the book they are reading offers valuable insight into living productive lives" (p. 79). As I mentioned in Chapter 1 when I introduced the narrative nonfiction spiral, this genre offers all sorts of avenues for further exploration through supporting texts. Many of the allusions identified through the collaborative chapter notes can lead to an ancillary text. For example, a pop culture reference might call for listening to a song or watching a film clip, or a notable historical event could prompt a news clip or article. Critical texts like reviews and interviews also offer valuable perspective on the anchor text and the broader text set.

When teachers curate supporting nonfiction texts, we provide students a broader lens and specific tools with which to better contextualize the anchor text. Students can also be charged with finding and sharing relevant supporting texts. The challenge lies in balancing the right amount of additional texts: enough to augment the unit but not so many that the focus on the anchor text is obscured.

The 1-1-1 Research Paper

While daily discussion and the previous activities allow for a vast range of topics to be explored, well-written narrative nonfiction novels often have several core themes or concepts that lend themselves to more focused research. I designed the 1-1-1 research paper assignment as an opportunity for students to explore these key topics. The 1-1-1 assignment is a mini-research paper with the numbers referring to one source, one citation or quote from that source, and one total page in length.

During previous research units, I noticed that students often had too many citations in rapid succession without explanation, or else they wrote long stretches of supposition without referencing a source. The idea behind the 1-1-1 assignment is to help students to identify a quality academic article or source (from a database like Gale or EBSCOhost), which changed their thinking or answered a question about one of the key topics, and then to properly contextualize and explain one citation from that source. This activity provides a nice bridge to our formal research unit (which follows the narrative nonfiction unit in my curricular sequence) where the skill of using context-citation-explanation within a longer research paper comes in handy.

Also, the brevity of this assignment makes it a fairly unobtrusive way for students to discover more about some of the anchor text's key topics without distracting them too much from the story. Students can easily share their 1-1-1 research papers with classmates in order to teach each other their newfound knowledge about key topics from the anchor texts. Figure 2.3 shows the instructions that I distribute to students for the 1-1-1 research paper along with a sample 1-1-1 paper that I wrote as an example for students.

Figure 2.3 The 1-1-1 Research Paper Student Description and Sample (MLA Format)

The 1-1-1 Research Paper

Because of its narrative nonfiction genre, *The Soloist* presents many avenues for further research, which we will address through the 1-1-1 research paper. This assignment will accomplish two purposes. The first is that it will allow us to gather and share more information on some of the key topics presented in the book. The second is that the 1-1-1 paper will be a building block tool for use during the research unit (our next major unit). The goal of this assignment is not to comprehensively explore a topic but rather to simply glean one useful fact, statistic, quote, etc. from one credible source, and then collectively (when we share with classmates), we'll have more background to apply to the context of the novel.

The **1-1-1 Research Paper** should consist of:

◆ **1 Source**: An article or report from Gale or of high academic caliber.
◆ **1 Citation** or Quote: One key piece from your source offering a new insight about your topic.
◆ **1 Page** in length, including the following parts:
  ● Introduction/Contextualization of the citation/quote: What does a reader basically need to understand in order to understand the citation?
  ● The citation itself in MLA format.
  ● Explanation of the significance of the citation in broader terms: What does the citation mean?

Topic Threads (inspired by *The Soloist*)—choose one of the following:

◆ Schizophrenia
  ● Causes, symptoms, treatments, prevention
◆ The connection between mental illness and homelessness
  ● Statistics, causes (why do the mentally ill become homeless?), laws/legislation, etc.
◆ Effective treatment of severe mental illness
  ● The balance of medication vs. psychotherapy (counseling)
  ● History of treatment (shock therapy, forced restraint and intake into facilities, etc.)
◆ The role of autonomy/self-rule/dignity with regards to severe mental illness
  ● When is it ethical and/or legal to treat someone against his/her will?
◆ The role/responsibility of the modern journalist to readers/society
  ● How is journalism changing in the digital age?
  ● How does profit/branding factor into the objectivity of the journalist?
◆ Beethoven
  ● His creative process
  ● His own personal struggles as a "tortured genius"

Example of a 1-1-1 Research Paper (Teacher-Created): Going Back Home: The Importance of Supported Post-Treatment Transition

A root word and question within the term "homelessness" is that of "home." How do people with mental illnesses come to be without a home? Did they have one and then lose it? Several common possibilities become apparent; perhaps a person was living with family or friends who became unwilling or unable to support the person's needs anymore. Perhaps the mental illness caused the person to be unable to continue working in order to pay rent, and the person was incapable of finding support services. Perhaps a homeless person with a mental illness spent time in a treatment facility with nowhere to go but back to the streets upon release.

Regardless of the original cause of homelessness, it's this last possibility that deserves further consideration. In order to end homelessness among the mentally ill, people facing both conditions (homelessness and mental illness) must receive help with both conditions. Sun writes in "Helping Homeless Individuals with Co-Occurring Disorders: the Four Components" that, "supported and permanent housing have a positive effect in combating chronic homelessness among people with mental disorders." In other words, if a mentally ill and homeless person receives treatment in a facility, in order for that person to stay off of the streets, he or she needs to have a place to live upon release.

In addressing a component of effective treatment, Sun likely identifies a reason that the mentally ill often become homeless. If a person spends a length of time, either voluntarily or involuntarily, in a treatment facility and then is released with no permanent home to go to, it's clear why the street becomes a last resort (especially for a person living with the strained and limited resources of a severe mental illness). Sun proves how complex these overlapping problems become. In order to "end" homelessness for the mentally ill, not only do they need psychological and/or psychiatric treatment for their illness, they also need a supported transition to a permanent home.

Works Cited

Sun, An-Pyng. "Helping homeless individuals with co-occurring disorders: the four components." *Social Work* 57.1

(2012): 23+. *General OneFile*. Web. 2 Mar. 2015.

Teacher Preparation while Students Read the Anchor Text

◆ Create a template for chapter notes using Google Docs or another collaborative platform and share this with student groups. Assign or have students select chapters from their reading to discuss and fill in, and then share the completed collaborative chapter notes document with the entire class. Have students refer to the completed document for further discussion or during future activities.

◆ Schedule appropriate times in the reading calendar to present supporting nonfiction texts. During which parts of the story and what parts of the discussion will the supporting texts be most beneficial? Since I primarily assign the reading of the anchor text as homework, I usually work the supporting texts into mini-lessons during class. Have students read, view, or listen to the text, discuss it for its own value and then tie it back to the anchor text.

◆ Coordinate discussion throughout the reading of the anchor text. Remember to conduct empathy check-ins to remind students of the authorial presence and encourage them to consider how portrayals of the narrator and characters affect reader reactions. Ask students what they are learning through the personal account and how the narrative structure facilitates that learning. It's also interesting to discuss how the elements of plot are affected in nonfiction. How can an author develop rising action, build to climactic moments, and offer resolutions with real-life events, especially considering that, in nonfiction, the plotline extends beyond the beginning and ending of the book?

◆ Identify topics for the 1-1-1 Research Paper assignment. What are the bigger concepts related to the novel that students could benefit from researching further? Make a list for students to choose from, and give them the option of identifying their own topic for research as well.

3. Post-Reading: Film Adaptation of Anchor Text

I remember my middle school and high school English teachers showing film versions of our curricular texts. We sometimes had good discussions about the overlap between book and film, but often these viewings felt more like short breathers before we transitioned to the next unit—a reward for students having read the book and a chance for the teacher to catch up on grading quizzes. When students are asked to actively engage with a book's film adaptation, however, it provides a powerful opportunity to work with the story on a new level. The multimodal combination of moving and still images, narration, music, and sound effects provides an experience that print text alone cannot.

During his 2015 keynote presentation at the National Board for Professional Teaching Standards' Teaching & Learning Conference, legendary documentary filmmaker Ken Burns noted that, while some lament the rise of a visual culture, "[t]his kind of visual literacy that our children are being raised on can be a kind of partner in the work we do that drives them then to books" (National Board for Professional Teaching Standards, 2015). Burns mentioned that each time one of his documentary series airs on PBS, book sales related to the series increase.

Such connection between visual and print literacy is especially important in narrative nonfiction because, on average, more viewers are going to see a film based on a nonfiction book than readers who will read the source material. Such adaptations are what Gutkind (2012) labeled "BOTS—based on a true story." Gutkind warned that "BOTS contain many factual elements but are mostly fiction" (p. 28). While these fictionalized elements may help a film's entertainment or commercial value and also solve the problem of how to squeeze a story that may have taken a reader weeks to read into a 2-hour viewing experience, mixing fiction and fact also causes problems. Zacks (2015) wrote, [s]tudies show that if you watch a film—even one concerning historical events about which you are informed—your beliefs may be reshaped by 'facts' that are not factual" (para. 4). The power of film is enough to make viewers believe cinematized truth over actual fact. However, "[h]aving the misinformation explicitly pointed out and corrected *at the time it was encountered* substantially reduced its influence" (Zacks, 2015, para. 13).

Watching the film version of a narrative nonfiction anchor text puts the student in the role of truth-detective. Asking students to identify and discuss what the filmmakers changed and what they got right allows the student to examine the rhetorical choices of editors and producers just as we examined the rhetorical choices of the author while reading the book. Hopefully, completing this activity for a book they now know well will also encourage students to take future BOTS films with a grain of salt (or better yet, to read the source texts).

When students ask why they have to read when they could just watch the movie instead, the answer lies in activities and discussion comparing and contrasting the film version with the anchor text.

Student Activities during Post-Reading

- ◆ Watch the film. As you watch, use a comparison/contrast t-chart to note what the film kept faithful to what was written in the book along with what was changed.
- ◆ As you list the differences, consider why the filmmakers changed these scenes or details from the book. Were the changes effective?
- ◆ Write a short evaluation of the film. Was it an effective interpretation of the anchor text or not? Did it add to or detract from the overall story? Draw on your comparison and contrast chart notes to discuss specific scenes that were done well and/or ones that were particularly problematic.

Teacher Preparation during Post-Reading

- ◆ Facilitate discussion around what students notice about the film. Point out any specifically strong film scenes that do a good job of bringing the book to life as well as the opposite. Which scenes are particularly ineffective? What "facts" do the filmmakers get wrong, and why might they make these changes?
- ◆ Consider inviting a guest speaker to engage your students on topics related to the anchor text. Skype and videoconferencing platforms makes it easier than ever to invite authors, or even real-life characters from the book into your classroom. If the author or a character is an impossible connection, then consider a connection in your local community. Who has expertise regarding the big topics and issues raised in your text set? I was lucky enough to have *The Soloist* author Steve Lopez talk with my class via Facetime (which I'll talk about further in Chapter 3), which encouraged a colleague who was reading *I am Malala* with her eighth graders to reach out to Malala's publicists with a similar invitation. Though Malala's people politely declined (since Malala wanted to remain focused on her schoolwork), my colleague was able to bring in a local Afghani military official (and a parent of one of her students) who was studying at the U.S. Army War College in our hometown, and he provided a personal and interactive perspective on the situation in Afghanistan relating to Malala's story.

What's endearing is that students usually report that they prefer the book over the movie after this activity. While the film offers unique visual and auditory vantage points, students also recognize that there's so much more story and information in a good narrative nonfiction book than can fit in a 2-hour film.

After finishing the pre-reading, anchor text, and post-reading sequence of the narrative nonfiction spiral, students are in a good position to reflect on the genre as a whole. Some of the questions I like to ask include: "What's one thing you learned from reading a narrative nonfiction book?" and "What can you get out of reading narrative nonfiction that you can't get out of other genres like fiction and poetry?" Some of my students' answers are featured in the Student Snapshots at the beginnings of Chapters 1, 2, and 3 of this book.

While the activities in this chapter would make a solid unit in and of themselves, they are further enhanced when students can try their hand at the genre by writing their own personal essays as a culminating assessment. Part II of this book, "Writing the Truth" picks up where these activities leave off to get students writing their own narrative nonfiction. Before we arrive there, however, Chapter 3 shows the narrative nonfiction spiral sequence in action with activities and sample student work from my tenth grade class for Steve Lopez's (2008) *The Soloist: A Lost Dream, and Unlikely Friendship, and the Redemptive Power of Music.*

Chapter

3

Sample Reading Unit:
The Soloist by Steve Lopez

Student Snapshots

What can you get out of reading narrative nonfiction that you can't get out of other genres like fiction or poetry?

"With narrative nonfiction, you see how the story can change based on who's telling it." Emma L.

"By reading the story of a real person with similar problems as you, you know you're not alone and that other people go through the same things as you." Tyler H.

What's one thing you learned from reading a narrative nonfiction book?

"Before reading the book, I knew that there was a homelessness problem, but I had no idea it was as big as described. I also didn't know that homelessness was so closely related to mental illness." Erik P.

"It takes a lot of effort and patience to gain and keep a friendship with someone with a mental illness or disorder. It can be very frustrating but at the same time very rewarding." Hannah M.

Two weeks after my tenth grade classes started reading *The Soloist: A Lost Dream, an Unlikely Friendship, and the Redemptive Power of Music*, I received an e-mail:

> Dear Mr. G,
> I do not want to finish reading Chapter 12. I am at the part where they are sitting and listening to the rehearsal and I can guarantee something bad will happen. I'm really mad at you for making us read this book because I don't want anything bad to happen to Nathaniel (even though I know it will). You're a cruel man. I guess I'll go finish the chapter.
>   Your Frustrated Student

After noting the hint of sarcasm in this e-mail, what I found more remarkable was that this student, who hadn't demonstrated much concern for previous literary characters, was engaged enough in this book to feel worried about the fate of one of its main characters. The e-mail was early evidence that we'd picked a narrative nonfiction book capable of hooking high school readers from a genre that most of my students reported not having read much of previously.

The Soloist details author Steve Lopez's friendship with Nathaniel Anthony Ayers, a classically trained musician who had once been admitted to Juilliard before symptoms of paranoid schizophrenia derailed a potential career as a professional musician (see Safer, 2009). Lopez meets Ayers, now homeless and living in Los Angeles, and what starts as the subject of Lopez's *L.A. Times* column grows into a unique friendship between the two men, which continues today. Part memoir and part literary journalism, *The Soloist* details 2 years in the lives of Lopez and Ayers along with relevant backstory from both characters. Through the personal story, *The Soloist* also explores the epidemic of homelessness and the link between mental illness (schizophrenia, specifically) and homelessness in the Skid Row section of Los Angeles. Through Nathaniel (and Lopez's struggle to offer meaningful support, help, and friendship to him), readers develop an appreciation of how massive and complex the interrelated issues of the book are.

Lopez began writing about Nathaniel and their budding friendship in his weekly column. As the column grew more popular and the story developed, he fleshed out the columns and filled in the blanks to create the book, which was then adapted into the 2009 film starring Robert

Downey, Jr. and Jamie Foxx as Lopez and Ayers, respectively. Since this text set perfectly matches the narrative nonfiction spiral pattern presented in Chapter 1, it also neatly sets up the pre-reading, anchor text, and post-reading sequence outlined in Chapter 2. Figure 3.1 shows the specific texts and major activities I used with my tenth grade classes for each step.

Figure 3.1 Sample Narrative Nonfiction Spiral Progression

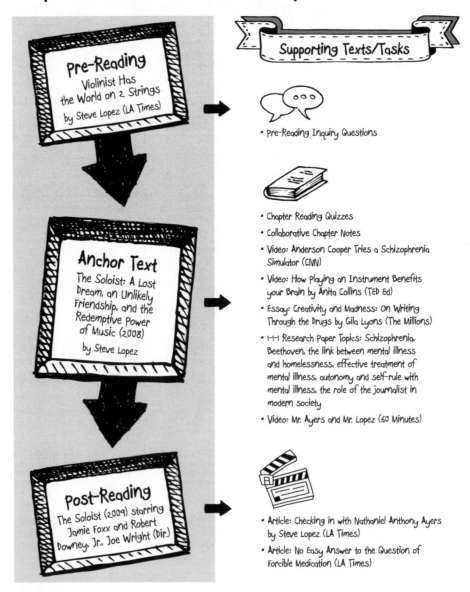

Sample Narrative Nonfiction Spiral Progression

Pre-Reading
Violinist Has the World on 2 Strings
by Steve Lopez (LA Times)

Supporting Texts/Tasks

• Pre-Reading Inquiry Questions

• Chapter Reading Quizzes
• Collaborative Chapter Notes
• Video: Anderson Cooper Tries a Schizophrenia Simulator (CNN)
• Video: How Playing an Instrument Benefits your Brain by Anita Collins (TED Ed)
• Essay: Creativity and Madness: On Writing Through the Drugs by Gila Lyons (The Millions)
• ꟷ Research Paper Topics: Schizophrenia, Beethoven, the link between mental illness and homelessness, effective treatment of mental illness, autonomy and self-rule with mental illness, the role of the journalist in modern society
• Video: Mr. Ayers and Mr. Lopez (60 Minutes)

Anchor Text
The Soloist: A Lost Dream, an Unlikely Friendship, and the Redemptive Power of Music (2008)
by Steve Lopez

Post-Reading
The Soloist (2009) starring Jamie Foxx and Robert Downey, Jr. Joe Wright (Dir.)

• Article: Checking in with Nathaniel Anthony Ayers by Steve Lopez (LA Times)
• Article: No Easy Answer to the Question of Forcible Medication (LA Times)

1. Pre-Reading: "Violinist has the World on 2 Strings" by Steve Lopez in the *Los Angeles Times*

To start, it made sense for students to read Lopez's first column, "Violinist has the World on 2 Strings." This short piece details the first time that Lopez meets Nathaniel and gives some basic story details that are later fleshed out in the opening chapters of the book. The article is a nice gateway into the overall story, and I asked students to read it and annotate it in any way they'd like, and then to address the following prompt:

> What do you want to know more about? List five questions you are curious about in response to the article (that you hope are answered or addressed in the book).

Students were intrigued by the column and asked insightful questions. I collected their questions and grouped them into a guide that we could refer back to while reading the novel. I also listed several "big" questions, which I hoped would be focal points for framing discussion throughout the entire unit. Figure 3.2 includes our collective list of questions.

Figure 3.2 Students' Pre-Reading Inquiry Questions Grouped into Categories and Several Framing 'Big' Questions for Continued Discussion

Questions about Nathaniel:

Why won't he accept money or strings?

Why isn't his sister involved in his life? Why doesn't his family try to help him? Did something happen between them?

How did his mom's death affect him? Did his mom get him into music?

How did he get his start as a musician?

How does he switch instruments so easily?

How does he memorize all his music? How does he remember phone numbers?

Why didn't Nathaniel go to his former teachers/classmates for help?

How did he go from Juilliard to the street?

If he's so talented, why doesn't he get a job or play with a local orchestra?

Has Nathaniel played any concerts since Juilliard?

What was his life like before the diagnosis?

Why won't he take medicine?

Did Nathaniel profit from the book about him?

Questions about Steve Lopez:

What is Steve's (the author's) role in this story? Is the author exploiting Nathaniel for profit?

Why did Lopez take such an interest in Nathaniel?

Does Lopez continue to seek Nathaniel's friendship?

Will the author help to get Nathaniel off of the street?

Will Lopez really be able to help him?

What was Lopez doing before he met Nathaniel?

Does Lopez have a passion for music? How did Lopez become a journalist for *The LA Times*?

Why does the author continue to talk to Nathaniel if he knows Nathaniel's schizophrenic?

How often did Lopez meet with Nathaniel?

Questions about schizophrenia:

What is schizophrenia? How did Nathaniel get it?

What causes schizophrenia?

What is schizophrenia's role in memory?

Are there different degrees of schizophrenia, and how bad does Nathaniel have it?

Does music have a positive effect on schizophrenia?

Questions about the book's plot:

Where is Nathaniel now? Does he ever get off the streets?

Is there a happy ending to this story?

Big Questions

- What is the role of the modern journalist in society? Are newspapers still relevant?
- Where are the ethical boundaries when it comes to writing about real people?
  - What are the challenges and benefits of presenting yourself as a character and/or narrating your own story?
  - Where are the ethical boundaries in telling someone else's story?
- What are the connections between mental illness and homelessness? What are the responsibilities of family members, friends, and even average citizens regarding people who are homeless and/or living with mental illness?
- What are the most effective treatments for mental illness? Which are the most ethical forms of treatment?
- What is the role of autonomy (self-rule) in the treatment of the mentally ill? Is it ever appropriate to force treatment or take away the freedom of another person?
- What is schizophrenia, and what can we reasonably hope for/expect from a person living with schizophrenia?

Contributing to this list of pre-reading inquiry questions generated curiosity and investment among my students. They were eager to start reading to find out how the plot unfolds between Lopez and Ayers, and they were also interested in learning more about schizophrenia, specifically.

We also talked generally about the genre of narrative nonfiction during this pre-reading stage. After supplying the two basic "rules" of the genre (1. The story has to be true, and 2. This true story is engaging and includes elements of plot), I asked students to consider the challenges and benefits of creating plot out of real-life events as well as the challenges and benefits of writing about real people. Figure 3.3 includes some of their responses.

Figure 3.3 Student Responses to Pre-Reading Narrative Nonfiction Genre Questions

What are the challenges of creating "plot" out of real-life events?	Any benefits?
• "Real-life is boring. There are no dragons or vampires in real life. There are no perfect moments. You have to tell it as it is and hope it sells." • "It may interest the writer but not be interesting to readers." • "It's hard to write about successes without sounding like you're bragging." • "Sometimes we can't recall exact details." • "You can't change what happened to make it more interesting."	• "No writer's block." • "Real events = bigger emotional impact." • "People can relate better to a true story." • "It's easier to write since there's already a sort of plotline to follow." • "You can add your perspective to make it more interesting without fabricating the actual events." • "You can research events to find out more."

What are the challenges/limitations of writing about real people?	Any benefits?
• "The people in the story could get offended by the way they're portrayed." • "You can't embellish their characteristics." • "You can't make up things they said or did to improve the story." • "You might be hesitant to invade their privacy by publishing about them." • "You might be biased against them or forget what they actually said." • "It's hard to make people as exciting on paper as they seem in real life."	• "If you get something wrong, someone will know." • "You can get other people's stories out into the world and make an impact." • "It's easy to describe their physical and personality traits." • "When people read fascinating things about real people, those things become even more exciting." • "Readers care more about real people." • "A variety of character types can confirm the truths of your story."

2. Anchor Text: *The Soloist: A Lost Dream, an Unlikely Friendship, and the Redemptive Power of Music* by Steve Lopez

As students began to read the anchor text, my primary goal during the first week of our reading calendar was just for them to get invested in the story. After assigning a few chapters to read each night, we'd start class with a quick five to ten question recall quiz. I'd use a review of the quiz answers to launch into a class discussion where we'd dig deeper into the events and questions from the chapter. As an additional resource to record and guide our conversations, I provided a chapter notes chart similar to the template in Figure 2.2. Since *The Soloist* includes so many references to songs, composers, and musicians, we added a "Playlist" column in addition to vocabulary, our "To Google" list (for non-musical allusions), and plot-based discussion questions.

The Playlist column added another modality with which to bring the book to life for students. When Lopez would mention them in the reading, I'd play YouTube clips of Yo-Yo Ma performing the Elgar Cello Concerto, Itzhak Perlman playing the Beethoven Violin Concerto, or even Stevie Wonder and Neil Diamond when they came up. As we got further into the reading calendar, I shifted more responsibility for the book's discussion and analysis onto my students.

Collaborative Chapter Notes

The Soloist is divided into three parts. As students read Part I, I provided information for our chapter notes, or I led a whole-group discussion to generate it. As we moved into Parts II and III of the book, I asked students to contribute to a blank chapter notes template using Google Docs. Groups of three or four students would select (or be assigned) a chapter and, after their initial independent reading, they'd work back through together to identify Playlist items, vocabulary, "To Google" allusions, and several plot-based discussion questions.

As student groups completed their chapters, they contributed a piece to a study guide with summary and analysis for the entire book that the rest of the class could then access for further consideration. Since I first developed this activity just as a way to engage students and democratize our conversation, I only asked students to look over their classmates' contributions after they were done, and then we'd incorporate them into our general class discussion. But, a number of useful follow-up activities could potentially come from collaborative chapter notes, including student-curated vocabulary quizzes, students responding to each other's discussion questions in writing, student-led class discussions, and more. It was neat to pull up the Google Doc on the Smart Board and watch as multiple groups completed their sections simultaneously.

Figure 3.4 shows an excerpt of students' collective work on our collaborative chapter notes document.

Figure 3.4 Collaborative Chapter Notes: Student Groups Added Notes for These Three Chapters to a Class Google Doc

Chapters	Playlist	Vocabulary	To Google (allusions)	Plot-Based Discussion Questions
22	None	Intractable (207) Euphoria (213) Reminiscing (213) Piques (210)	Big Brothers, Big Sisters (211) Road to Recovery by Mark Ragins (209) Formula 409 Cleaner (208) Google (213) Gulf War (213) Muscovites (213)	Do you think music therapy is effective? Why or why not? Do you agree with Ragins' theory that the relationship is more important than the medicine? Why doesn't Steve Lopez have other friends? Why was Lopez's wife so against him switching jobs?
23	Bach Prelude No.1 Bloch Prayer Schubert Arpeggione Saint-Saëns	fracas (219) gabby (220) soliloquy (222) enclave (223) squalor (223)	Echo Park (219) Los Angeles River (219) Union Rescue Mission (219) La Guardia Airport, JFK (221) Yo-Yo Ma (221) Prince of Denmark (222) Griffith Observatory (223) Hermann Hesse (223)	Do you think that Nathaniel wants a family of his own? What does Nathaniel's behavior around Caroline and Lopez's family reveal about his own childhood and family life? Do you think that Lopez was scared of Nathaniel meeting Caroline?
24	Serenade in D major Op. 8	belligerent (228) brassiere (226) erudite (227) caravan (230)	Los Angeles Philharmonic (224) Disney Hall (225) Mr. White/whitefacing (226)	Do you think Lopez exploits Nathaniel? Will Nathaniel ever find love?

(continued overleaf)

Figure 3.4 Continued

Chapters	Playlist	Vocabulary	To Google (allusions)	Plot-Based Discussion Questions
	Piano Trio No. 3 in C minor, Op. I, No. 3 Spring Quartet No. 5 in A major, Op. 18, No. 5 (224–225) Beethoven's Fifth and Eighth Symphonies (225)		white plague, bubonic plague, sickle-cell anemia (228) President Bush's homeless czar (229) Midnight Mission (229) Philip Mangano (229) Zev Yaroslavsky (230) Swastika (226)	What are the flaws of the mayor's approach to homelessness? How would you improve on his plan?

Empathy Check-Ins

Lopez (2008) wrote in *The Soloist* that, "I've set a trap for myself without knowing it, and readers aren't letting me forget it . . . in telling Nathaniel's story, I have unwittingly taken on some responsibility for his welfare, a job I am clearly, demonstrably and undeniably unqualified for" (p. 27). One aspect of Lopez's narration that I appreciate is how he demonstrated awareness, through passages like this, of both how delicate it is to share his own thoughts and actions as well as to tell someone else's story, when both are subjected to public judgment once a story is published. Lopez reveals his missteps, mistakes, and doubts and, in doing so, he no doubt opens himself to judgment from readers. Critically examining the author's choices and how those affect reader response is exactly the point of empathy check-ins.

Building on the general questions I asked students during the pre-reading phase about the challenges and benefits of writing about real people, I asked students to tell me what they thought about Lopez and Nathaniel at several specific points in our reading. These empathy check-ins invited students to examine the rhetorical choices of the author. What did Lopez do that made them trust him (or not) and care about Nathaniel (or not)? In fact, the student e-mail at the beginning of this chapter was an unsolicited empathy check-in. In it, the student revealed his fondness for Nathaniel which made him more invested in reading further (despite his sense of dread that something bad would happen).

Figure 3.5 shows examples of my students' responses when, about halfway through our reading of the book, I asked them if they cared what happened to Nathaniel and what they thought of Lopez. While

Figure 3.5 Sample Empathy Check-Ins: Student Responses Show Engagement with How the Narrator and Characters were Portrayed in the Book

Do you care what happens to Nathaniel? Why or why not?
• "Yes. Nathaniel is still a human being. He can feel pain, loneliness, etc., and he's already been through so much because of his illness. He just wants to play music, and I hope nothing bad happens to him. He's a likeable and innocent person with an innocent dream. He really doesn't deserve to be hurt anymore."
• "Yes, because we are so embedded in his life. Nathaniel interests me not only for his talent, but he's intelligent, wise, experienced, and polite, all of which make me like him more. I'd like to believe that I like Nathaniel genuinely because of his characteristics and not out of pity."
• "Yes, I do care about what happens to Nathaniel. I can get easily attached to characters in books, but Nathaniel is real and therefore is an even more powerful character. My family has a history of mental illness too, and I am pre-disposed to both depression and bi-polar disorder. Mental illness really hits home for me which is part of why I care about Nathaniel."
• "At first, I did not really care about what happened to Nathaniel, but now I do. While reading this book, we have become attached to Lopez and Nathaniel like characters in a novel, and we feel connected to them more than if we would have just read a news article. My first opinion was that Nathaniel was a good guy and I wanted him to succeed, but not necessarily more than any other homeless person I have passed. Now I feel that I have a connection to Nathaniel, and I wish him to succeed as I would a friend."
• "I do care what happens to Nathaniel. Hearing his back story has made me realize what he has lost, and I hope to see him recover in some form. Lopez's portrayal of him has a strong sense of reality, which makes me connect a lot with the character. Seeing the small amounts of progress he has made has made me want to see him improve more and more. Overall, I care strongly about what happens to Nathaniel mostly because of how real his character is."

What do you think of Steve Lopez at this point in the book?
• "I think he's really trying to be a good person. He seriously wants to help Nathaniel but doesn't know how. And even though he's struggling, he's still persevering and getting more involved in Nathaniel's life. Lopez complains a few times, but he's only human. We all have our own limits. I still think he's a good guy."
• "I honestly think that Steve cares for Nathaniel. Although his original intention was to find a story, I think that he has grown closer to Nathaniel and views him as a friend he wants to help."
• "I've always thought that Lopez's intentions were true, even if everything that's happened may not have been intentional. You can tell he is a good person because he is able to recognize that he's in over his head, yet he still doesn't let down Nathaniel."

(continued overleaf)

Figure 3.5 Continued

What do you think of Steve Lopez at this point in the book?
• "I think that Steve Lopez is pretty selfish due to the fact that most of the time he is focused on how good of an article each event would make. He also seems like he wants to leave but feels obligated to stay due to social pressure to make sure Nathaniel gets back on his feet." • "At first, I was not fond of Lopez. I thought he only used Nathaniel for his story, and that he's writing of the toll that Nathaniel took on his life to portray himself as a Good Samaritan. However, although natural skepticism still lingers, I have grown more approving of Lopez now that the story turned more into one about the inequalities of mental illness." • "I think Lopez is a man who bit off more than he can chew, but is handling the situation well. It reflects well on his character that he was willing to try and help Nathaniel even after realizing the full extent of his issues."

students were almost universally concerned about Nathaniel's fate, they had mixed feelings about the author with some students labeling him as selfish or describing him as opportunistic. I found this contrast ironic since readers wouldn't know anything about Nathaniel if it weren't for Lopez's book. Pointing out this irony to students made for a great class discussion that might only be possible through the genre of narrative nonfiction.

At a writer's conference, I heard an author talk about how she carefully cataloged comments and reviews of her memoir. She noted that about a third of the reviewers liked her as a narrator and agreed with her course of actions in the book. Another third of the reviewers disliked her as a narrator but agreed with her course of actions. The final third of reviewers both disliked her as a narrator and disagreed with her course of actions. The writer used her observation to talk about how difficult it is to "go public" and write yourself as a narrator or present yourself as a character in narrative nonfiction. This writer's anecdote prompts some interesting questions regarding the relationship between likeability and trustability of a narrator.

When students finished reading *The Soloist*, I asked them to complete one final empathy check-in with several related questions. The first was whether they liked Lopez after reading his book and his supporting columns. The second was, regardless of their answer to the first, whether they trusted him as a narrator. Then, I asked students to consider whether it was important to like and/or trust a narrator while reading narrative nonfiction. Figure 3.6 shows some of their responses to those questions.

Figure 3.6 Narrating Nonfiction: Building off the Periodic Empathy Check-Ins, Students Explore the Narrator's Self-Portrayal after Reading the Entire Book

---

1. After reading all of *The Soloist* as well as the additional columns, do you like Steve Lopez (as he presented himself in writing)? Why or why not?

- "I think Steve Lopez is a pretty likeable person. Not all of his actions in *The Soloist* were necessarily right or the same thing that I would have done, but that just makes him human. He presented himself in an honest way."
- "Honestly, I can't exactly decide if I like him or not. I don't agree with everything he does, but I do think he is a good person with mostly good intentions."
- "I like how Steve Lopez presented himself in his writing because it seemed like he didn't leave out anything."
- "I enjoy the fact that he tried not to glorify himself/make himself seem like a perfect savior. He emphasized the fact that he didn't have all the answers."

---

2. Regardless of your answer to #1, do you trust Lopez as a narrator? In other words if you grant him the bias and limited perspective of a first-person narrator, do you believe he gave you an honest and fair account of his feelings and experiences throughout the book? Why or why not?

- "I trust Lopez as a narrator because he was very open and honest about his actions and through process during the book's events. He showed his dilemmas and points in the action where he was unsure about what to do, followed by his ultimate decision and justification."
- "Yes, I trust Lopez as a narrator. Throughout the novel, he seemed to give a fair and reliable account of the events, even if they made him look bad. Also, most of the details in the novel can be proven and backed-up. He's a journalist, so it can be assumed that he would be honest."
- "I trust him to a certain extent. You could see into his mind, so to speak, but I feel like only three quarters of his thoughts were there. He would tell the truth, but not the whole truth, in other words."
- I do, because the book lines up well with reality. He didn't pretend to know everything about Nathaniel or his condition, and he presented himself as open to criticism."

---

3. In your opinion, is it important to like a narrator, and does this likeability factor into how much you trust him or her?

- "I think it's important to like a narrator just as it is important to like a character. If you don't like the characters, you're not likely going to enjoy the story. If you like the narrator, I think you are definitely going to be inclined to trust them, but when it comes to a book and people you don't know personally, trusting someone personally is different than trusting a narrator."
- "No, it's not important to like a narrator. A reader can like a narrator without agreeing with every choice he or she makes just like a reader can dislike a narrator and still agree with decisions."
- "I think it's nice, but not essential to like a narrator. His or her job isn't to be likeable, it's to tell a story. While Lopez didn't always make the best choices and some readers may not have liked him, he is very easy to trust and comes off as reliable. His background in journalism enhances his trustworthiness and make it less important for him to be liked."
- "I feel that liking a narrator makes the reader want to believe them more than if they didn't like the narrator. Disliking a narrator makes you more critical of their piece, which makes you more likely to be suspicious of their work."

Supporting Nonfiction

Because of the intersecting topics of music, creativity, mental illness, home-lessness, etc., *The Soloist* lent itself well to bringing in ancillary nonfiction pieces of various genres and modalities. I've already mentioned that I would show YouTube clips of musical performances that we had logged in the Playlist column of our chapter notes. I also selected articles and videos that might help to answer some of the students' question from our pre-reading list that went beyond the book.

One of the most effective activities involving supporting nonfiction was when I showed students the video "Anderson Cooper Tries a Schizo-phrenia Simulator" (Cooper, 2014), which features the CNN host donning headphones that pipe voices similar to what schizophrenics might hear into his ears as he tries to go about his daily tasks. Then, I showed Anita Collins' video "How Playing an Instrument Benefits your Brain" from TED-Ed (Collins, 2014), which uses animation to show that playing a musical instrument engages many regions of your brain simultaneously.

One of my students' enduring questions throughout the book is why Nathaniel chooses to live on the streets and in a noisy tunnel rather than in a quiet apartment that becomes available for him at a local shelter. After watching the CNN video, students speculated that the noise of the streets and the tunnel might distract Nathaniel from the voices in his head and that the quiet of an apartment might actually serve to amplify those inner voices. Furthermore, students suggested, after watching the TED-Ed video, that playing music might engage more of Nathaniel's brain, which, in turn, limits his brain from generating voices and paranoia. Through the videos, students came to better understand Nathaniel's idiosyncrasies and how music could be therapeutic for him. While the book itself does explain these findings to a point, the ancillary nonfiction helped students to connect the dots.

Another effective ancillary nonfiction source was Gila Lyons' essay "Creativity and Madness: On Writing through the Drugs" (Lyons, 2014). As the title suggests, Lyons explores the connection between creativity and madness, and then she shares that, although they do indeed dull her creativity and writing ability, she elects to take the medication prescribed by her psychiatrist because of its overall benefit to her life. Lyons' essay provided perspective as students wrestled with the issue of forced medica-tion in treating mental illness. In *The Soloist*, Nathaniel is reluctant to take medication because he wants to retain his autonomy, he worries about medication dulling his musical ability, and because he's had negative effects from medication in the past.

Gallagher (2009) wrote:

> The value in teaching this book is not simply to provide our students with a slice of cultural literacy or to teach them to recognize literary elements such as foreshadowing. The value comes when we use this great book as a springboard to examine issues in today's world. (p. 66)

Short ancillary nonfiction sources like videos and essays better allow students to connect the issues from the book with the issues in other real-life contexts. However, this learning happens thanks to *both* the reading of the book *and* the reading of short nonfiction pieces. The sources are complementary, and the learning, which would not be as potent from just reading a book *or* just reading nonfiction articles, is more effective because of the combination.

As we were reading *The Soloist*, a homeless man was shot and killed by police in LA's Skid Row. The police were responding to a call about a possible robbery, and when they made contact with the man, he reportedly grabbed for one of their weapons, which caused the other officers to open fire. Because we had been reading about homelessness and Skid Row in the book, students paid extra attention to this news and brought it to my attention. In class, we watched the news coverage and read updates as they became available. Our work with the book gave us a vessel to process and discuss this tragic current event, and students were equipped with background information in order to better understand the broader and complex circumstances surrounding it. While they certainly can't be predicted or planned for, current events can often be brought into literary discussion, and the curricular literature and previous class discussion may provide a foundation to discuss controversial events in a way that feels safe and productive to students and their teachers.

Finally, when my students finished reading *The Soloist*, three more short pieces of supporting nonfiction added a nice epilogue to the anchor text and an effective transition to the post-reading activity of watching the film adaptation. The first was a *60-Minutes* clip, which shows Steve Lopez and Nathaniel Ayers together and gives a brief account of their story (Safer, 2009). I knew that there were many pictures and videos of Lopez and Ayers only a Google search away, but I intentionally saved this clip for the end so that students could first picture the characters through the book's description and, for many students, the clip was the first time they saw both men and heard Nathaniel playing (though I'm sure some Googled them along the way).

Also, as we talked about in our class discussions, the plot lines of real, living people stretch beyond the beginning and end of narrative nonfiction books. Lopez wrote several more recent columns updating readers on Nathaniel's progress and their continuing friendship, so students read "Checking in with Nathaniel Ayers" (Lopez, 2014a) and "No Easy Answer to the Question of Forcible Medication" (Lopez, 2014b) as an epilogue to the book as well as additional chapters in the ongoing stories of Ayers and Lopez.

The 1-1-1 Research Paper

As I mentioned in Chapter 2, my goal in assigning the 1-1-1 research paper was to encourage students to better contextualize a citation from research. After reading too many student research papers that had either too many citations in a row with little explanation, or pages and pages of explanation with no citations, I created this brief assignment where students would contextualize and explain one citation from one source in less than one page. Mastering this contextualization would be a building block for students to apply to longer research projects with multiple sources in the future. Within this narrative nonfiction unit, the 1-1-1 research paper also gave students an opportunity to learn more about some of the key topics from *The Soloist*.

Following the instructions I presented in Figure 2.2, students selected from the topics of schizophrenia, the connection between mental illness and homelessness, effective treatment of mental illness (including the role of autonomy in treatment), the role and responsibilities of modern journalists, and Beethoven (one of Nathaniel's obsessions and, arguably, another mad genius). Next, they found an academic source using the Gale databases through our school library (or sources of an equivalent caliber found elsewhere). Finally, they contextualized and explained one key quote from the source in one page.

By and large, the short sequence and simple requirements of this assignment led to students completing it successfully, and it was also a helpful stepping stone for writing longer research papers incorporating multiple sources. Students drew from the pattern of "introduce, cite, and explain (repeat)" that they used in the 1-1-1 research paper in their longer research projects as well.

Figure 3.7 shows an example of a student 1-1-1 research paper where the author focused on creativity as an effective element in the treatment of mental illness.

Figure 3.7 Sample Student 1-1-1 Research Paper

Using Creativity as a Treatment for Mental Illnesses

The issue of treating mental illness patients with psychoactive drugs and medication has been a long term debate. Most doctors and physicians treat mental illnesses just like other biological illnesses, with drugs. This method often results in side effects, and it helps patients to keep going rather than directly curing the problem. Different treatments to mental illnesses such as therapy are also used, but they are not always taken advantage of in certain situations. Another alternative treatment method can be taken care of just by the patient alone. Many people don't recognize this, but those with "creative" minds, they can use their creativity and talent to put a stall on mental illnesses such as schizophrenia.

This alternative treatment can be extremely helpful and beneficial to those who are against the use of drugs, even though the mental illness is not directly addressed. In Scott Kaufman's article, "The Real Link Between Creativity and Mental Illness," he states that, "research shows that expressive writing increases immune system functioning, and the emerging field of posttraumatic growth is showing how people can turn adversity into creative growth." Strictly speaking, allowing one to explore their inner creativity helps to nullify the effects of mental illnesses such as schizophrenia. Also, these mental illnesses can be a strength in some cases that can yield creative geniuses such as artists and musicians.

In Kaufman's article, he directly relates the creative mind as a method of treating mental illnesses. While there are other methods out there to be used, there are those mental illness patients who would prefer to not use drugs or have to interact with certain people as a lifeline. This allows people to treat themselves slowly but surely through creativity by allowing their mind to flow freely. Using creativity as a treatment also enables individuals who suffer from mental illnesses to avoid the side effects of psychoactive drugs, and help retain the original emotions of their person.

Works Cited

Kaufman, Scott. "The Real Link between Creativity and Mental Illness." Scientific American. 3 Oct. 2013. Web. 16 Mar. 2015.

---

3. Post-Reading: *The Soloist* (2009 Film Adaptation)

In all honesty, the film version of *The Soloist* is not a great movie. Like most "based on a true story" adaptations, the film omits certain scenes and characters from the book, combines others, and even introduces characters and events not found in the source text. These and other directorial and production choices combine to earn a paltry 56 percent "Liked It" rating on Rotten Tomatoes' Tomatometer (Rotten Tomatoes, 2009).

Still, there are some bright spots. Jamie Foxx's portrayal of Nathaniel is well done. Foxx is able to capture the duality of Nathaniel's brilliance and illness in a way that viewers can comprehend. Several film scenes also vividly capture Lopez's description from the book. For example, Lopez described a night he spent with Nathaniel on Skid Row. He wrote:

> At Fourth and Los Angeles, a man lurks in a doorway with product for sale, and he's got his antenna up to make me as customer or cop. I haven't shaved and I'm wearing jeans, sneakers and a ball cap, a getup I think might help me blend in, but in truth I stand out like a tourist in Amish Country. You can't look at anyone here. It's a giveaway. You light the crack pipe, hire the hooker or get out of Dodge. I'm fooling no one, and suspicious eyes track my every step. On the corner, a Dumpster reeks of rotten food and dead flesh. The daytime bustle of Toy District commerce disappears as darkness and indifference grow. The last drafts of sunbaked urine rise off of stained asphalt and concrete. All systems are down and this place smells of doom. (2008, pp. 61–62)

As Robert Downey, Jr. (portraying Lopez) walks down a menacing Skid Row street in the film, it's clear that the filmmakers consulted the text closely, and this is a notable point of comparison for students. An interesting side-note (from reading articles about the film's production) is that filmmakers hired actual homeless people from Skid Row to portray themselves in this scene in the film.

There are also several scenes that are arguably more effective on film than they are in print. One example features Nathaniel in his apartment. Through a montage of sounds and images, viewers can see and hear that the apartment is overtly quiet to others, but to Nathaniel, the "quiet" space is filled with auditory hallucinations because of his schizophrenia.

And then there are the scenes and features that aren't effective. The film includes several strange plot points not found in the book, including Lopez battling raccoons by pouring coyote urine around his garden or being rushed to the emergency room after a bike wreck. I suspected (and a Google search confirmed) that these scenes actually came from other columns Lopez had written for the *LA Times* before he began writing about Nathaniel. In the context of the film, though, they seem disjointed.

In order to encourage students to engage critically with the film, I asked them to note similarities and differences with the book on a comparison/ contrast t-chart as they watched. Most students easily filled the front and back of a chart with an extensive list in both columns during the film. Figure 3.8 includes part of one student's t-chart from this activity.

Figure 3.8 Examining a BOTS (Based on a True Story) Film

Examining a BOTS (Based on a True Story) Film

Directions: As you watch the movie version of *The Soloist*, keep a running list of things that the filmmakers were faithful to and kept the same as the book (on the left) and note any changes/differences (on the right). Keep in mind that any changes the filmmakers made were done intentionally (for better or for worse). We'll discuss your reactions after we finish the film.

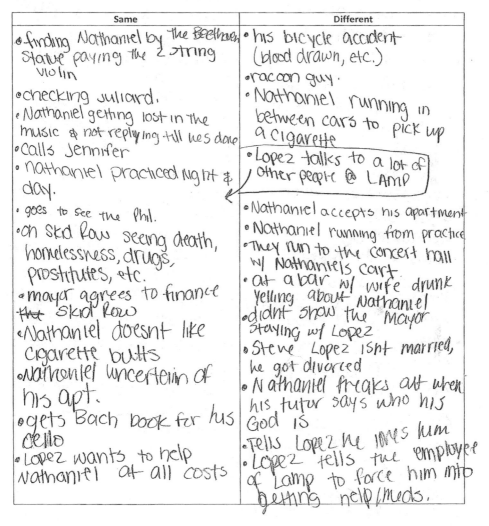

Same	Different
• finding Nathaniel by The Beethoven Statue playing the 2 string violin	• his bicycle accident (blood drawn, etc.)
• checking Juliard.	• racoon guy.
• Nathaniel getting lost in the music & not replying till he's done	• Nathaniel running in between cars to pick up a cigarette
• Calls Jennifer	• Lopez talks to a lot of other people @ LAMP
• Nathaniel practiced night & day.	
• goes to see the Phil.	• Nathaniel accepts his apartment
• on Skid Row seeing death, homelessness, drugs, prostitutes, etc.	• Nathaniel running from practice
• mayor agrees to finance that Skid Row	• They run to the concert hall w/ Nathaniel's cart
• Nathaniel doesnt like cigarette butts	• at a bar w/ wife drunk yelling about Nathaniel
• Nathaniel uncertain of his apt.	• didnt show the mayor staying w/ Lopez
• gets Bach book for his cello	• Steve Lopez isnt married, he got divorced
• Lopez wants to help Nathaniel at all costs	• Nathaniel freaks out when his tutor says who his God is
	• Tells Lopez he loves him
	• Lopez tells the employee of Lamp to force him into getting help/meds.

After they finished watching the film, I asked students to draw from their comparisons and contrasts to evaluate the effectiveness of the film by asking them what the film got right, what the film got wrong, and about their overall evaluation of the film adaptation. Figure 3.9 includes some of their responses.

Figure 3.9 Student Reactions to the Film Adaptation of *The Soloist*

What did the film get right/do well?

- "The film captured the heart of the music a lot better than a book ever could."
- "How Nathaniel's mind works and his rants."
- "Nathaniel's appearance, Skid Row, and Steve and Nathaniel's relationship (for the most part)."
- "It showed how pressured Lopez was from his deadlines."
- "Some of the same dialogue, depictions of Skid Row, schizophrenia, and some of the main scenes."
- "It captured Nathaniel's problem in a way that viewers could understand and had interesting points such as Nathaniel stopping and starting again, much to Lopez's disappointment."
- "Music and soundtrack, flashbacks, and the visual representations of real places."
- "It gave me insight into Nathaniel's past and why he is the way his is now (through flashbacks)."

What did the film get wrong/do poorly?

- "Getting Nathaniel to go inside the apartment seemed to go a lot quicker than in the book."
- "Some minor facts, like Steve Lopez being divorced."
- "The movie focused more on Lopez than Nathaniel."
- "The film added some extra scenes for comedy and audience appeal. Also, they made Steve Lopez seem like a harsh man who didn't have his life together, unlike in the book and in real life."
- "I think the film left out at least one crucial point which was the Yo-Yo Ma meet-up and dinner with Lopez's family."
- "The 'you are my God' scene was unnecessary and unfaithful to the book."
- "The bike crash, raccoon stuff, and ex-wife weren't in the book."
- "Several characters were misrepresented or excluded and Robert Downey, Jr. was a poor representation of Lopez."

Accepting that this is an adaptation (a "BOTS"), what is your overall impression of the film (good, bad, in between), and why do you feel this way?

- "Bad. I don't like Lopez in the movie at all. I also didn't like how Lopez seemed more important than Nathaniel multiple times in the movie."
- "It was okay. If I hadn't read the book, I would have liked it better. They did a good job portraying Nathaniel's schizophrenia and Skid Row, but they made Steve Lopez seem like a jerk, and after speaking to him via FaceTime, he's not like the movie version at all."
- "I think I'm more in between. As we discussed, it's difficult turning a book (or any story) into a film. There were things they definitely could have improved, but there were also parts that were really good. Overall, they got the message down, and that's the important part."
- "There were some very powerful moments in the film and even though it was not as good as the book, I still think it was a good movie."
- "I don't think that the film was as bad as everyone in my class thinks it is. I thought it helped me to visualize Nathaniel, Skid Row, and the voices Nathaniel hears. It wasn't true to the book but it displayed the dialogue and situations well for the given time frame."

Besides demonstrating to students directly how BOTS films are often fictionalized (which hopefully makes them critical viewers of other BOTS films where they don't read the source book), these evaluative activities led to productive discussion. When students would note differences between film and book, I'd challenge them to consider why the filmmakers made those changes. For example, one student pointed out a scene in the film where, in a bar, Lopez's ex-wife questions his motives for helping Nathaniel. The student noted that, since the real Lopez was married in the book, the character of the ex-wife was likely a composite who voiced dialogue in this one film scene from multiple characters and scenes in the book including from Lopez's wife, from Lopez's own inner-dialogue, and from a critic at a public speaking event. While the student didn't think this change was particularly effective, he understood why filmmakers made the change.

4. A Conversation with Steve Lopez

As I mentioned in Chapter 1, when I described my rationale for including a contemporary narrative nonfiction book in our curriculum, most of the books approved for my grade level were old fiction, which also meant that the authors were dead. As we talked more in this unit about how Lopez and Nathaniel were real, living people whose lives extended beyond the "plot" captured in the book, I also wondered what insights and updates Lopez would share with us personally if we had the chance to talk to him. Considering that he's still an *LA Times* reporter, his e-mail address was listed publicly in the byline of his articles. On a whim, and not really expecting a response, I sent him an e-mail, described our unit and work with his book and columns, and asked him if he'd be willing to Skype in to talk with my students.

To my surprise, he wrote back almost right away and told me he had relatives who lived close to our southcentral Pennsylvania high school. He didn't have Skype, but if we could figure out how to use Apple FaceTime, he was in. With the help of my district's technology department, we were able to set it up, and for 40 minutes, Lopez told behind-the-scenes stories, showed us photos, and answered student questions (see Payne, 2015). He told us that he and Nathaniel were invited to visit the White House and that Nathaniel dressed in an all-white suit for the occasion. He asked what the population of our town was (answer: about 19,000 people), and he noted that the homeless population in Los Angeles was over three times that number. Lopez ended by charging students with helping to end the stigma surrounding mental illness in order to work toward solutions.

Being able to interact with Lopez was clearly meaningful to my students. One of them wrote about the experience, "It made the whole thing seem a lot more real. Sometimes when reading, you can't fully grasp that an event actually happened, but, through hearing Lopez talk about meeting Nathaniel, it added even more depth to the story." Another student remarked in class after the facetime session that, "It's like we encountered three different versions of Steve Lopez . . . there was the one in the book, the one from the movie, and then the actual guy who we FaceTimed with." This insightful comment offered a unique teachable moment of critical analysis, and I followed up by asking the class which Lopez was "most real." They obviously ranked the movie version as most fictional, the book version was in the middle, and the FaceTime version was most real, but they recognized that there were rhetorical choices made in terms of how Lopez presented himself (or was presented) in each incarnation.

While it might not be possible for every teacher to Skype with an author, there may be other local experts who could interact with students about content from the anchor text. My backup guest if Lopez wasn't available was a friend who's a social worker and psychologist and has worked with people suffering from schizophrenia. He would have been able to answer students' questions about the illness and possibilities for treatment. I also considered contacting staff at our local homeless shelter to come and talk with students about the homelessness in our own community.

I didn't get permission from Lopez's publisher to air the full FaceTime video, but there's a brief clip of the conversation including some student reaction at: https://www.youtube.com/watch?v=Lj24H6ZWw9g. One of my students, a reporter for the school newspaper, also wrote an article about our conversation with Lopez and interviewed some of her classmates for their reactions: http://tinyurl.com/zx6j99g

The student work and perspective featured in this chapter demonstrate the broad value of incorporating a narrative nonfiction text set based on the spiral pattern presented in Chapter 1. In addition to the featured work, I also surveyed students at the end of the unit about what they learned from reading narrative nonfiction as well as the unique literary qualities of the genre. Some of their responses appear in the "Student Snapshots," which begin Chapters 1 to 3.

Part

II

Writing the Truth

Interlude

Why Write Personal Essays? A Case for Creative Writing as Reading Assessment

"You know, by the time they reach fifth grade, they pretty much know how to write a story." A few years ago, our director of curriculum and instruction explained to our department why we'd be minimizing the role of narrative writing in favor of informational and persuasive writing in our middle school ELA curriculum. The pre-Common Core eighth grade state writing test in Pennsylvania included only informational and persuasive prompts and, as the modern adage declares, "that which is not tested is not taught."

Around this same time, our English department chair, a former librarian and teacher, no less, declared that our department would no longer need to teach full-length novels since, "Nobody reads books anymore. Most people just read short articles on the internet, so that's what we should be teaching." Perhaps it's needless to say that our administrators' attitudes toward literacy instruction rankled me and some of my colleagues. However, considering the national dialogue surrounding the early days of the Common Core, such attitudes shouldn't have been surprising.

In a now infamous speech to the New York State Education Department, College Board president and Common Core "architect" David Coleman said:

> The only problem, forgive me for saying this so bluntly, the only problem with [personal writing] is as you grow up in this world you realize people really don't give a shit about what you feel or what you think. What they instead care about is can you make an argument with evidence, is there something verifiable behind what you're saying or what you think or feel that you can demonstrate to me. (2011, p. 22)

There is some merit in Coleman's statement; constructing evidence-based arguments is an important skill for students to master, but his broad dismissal of personal writing is problematic for several reasons. First, as I mentioned in Chapter 1, the literary landscape disputes Coleman's claim. The popularity of *Serial*, *The Moth*, *This American Life* and other narrative nonfiction podcasts, the many notable memoirs and works of literary non-fiction that continue to be adapted into based-on-a-true story films, and television shows like "Making a Murderer" prove that readers, viewers, and listeners are hungry for true, personal writing in various modalities.

Also, writing personally and constructing arguments are not mutually exclusive. TED talks are a potent example of how information and argu-ment are often powerfully encapsulated in first-person narratives. As I cited in Chapter 1, *Creative Nonfiction* magazine editor Lee Gutkind often references evidence that readers remember more facts for a longer dura-tion when those facts are encapsulated in personal stories. Perhaps Mr. Coleman has never had occasion to shop for a new car and encounter a well-crafted pitch from a salesperson, but the testimonial, loaded with personal thought and feeling, is a powerful tool for use in sales, advertis-ing, and other rhetorical forms. Newkirk (2014) suggested that the separa-tion between narrative, informative, and persuasive writing is an error in categorization. He wrote, "[n]arrative is a form or mode of discourse that can be used for multiple purposes . . . we use it to inform, to persuade, to entertain, to express. It is the 'mother of all modes,' a powerful and innate form of understanding" (p. 6).

Coleman's quote, along with the attitudes of my local administrators, demonstrates a phenomenon that Penny Kittle (2014) labeled "narrative disrespect" (p. 4), or the general idea that narrative is easy or unimportant writing. Kittle stated, "[a]nyone who thinks [narrative] is easy hasn't written a single story in a very long time. Perhaps ever" (p. 5). And besides being difficult, learning to craft well-written stories, especially personal ones, is important. Besides the reasons already mentioned, one of the gateway genres students need to master for college admittance is the college essay, a form of personal writing where creative nonfiction skills are quite useful.

Dean (2006) wrote, "By definition, genre is discourse that arises out of recurring communicative acts in certain social situations," and that, "Under-standing genre requires some understanding of the social context it arises from as well as an ability to read a text with certain considerations of the social nature of its context in mind" (p. 54). Early and DeCosta (2012) echoed Dean's comments on genre with, "the more experience students have with various real world writing tasks, the more they learn to comfortably navi-gate diverse forms of writing in different and important social contexts"

(p. 20). Learning to write well in specific genres like the college essay and the personal essay requires explicit instruction. For that matter, writing short fiction and poetry helps students to master the conventions of those genres. A major argument supporting the teaching of creative and personal writing is the benefit such writing can provide for reading ability.

So far, every set of standards that I've encountered during my teaching career, including the Common Core, charges English teachers with teaching literary elements from multiple genres. Kittle (2014) asked, "What better way to deeply understand the craft of scenes and the development of plot—the problematic relationships between characters and the layering of values, beliefs, and ideas in literature—than to study some and craft their own?" (p. 5). By making strategic decisions as writers and working with the literary elements and conventions of a specific genre, students develop a level of experiential knowledge that they could not necessarily gain through reading alone. Graham and Hebert (2010) confirmed that, "[s]tudents' reading skills and comprehension are improved by learning the skills and processes that go into creating text" (p. 5).

Of course, the link between writing and reading abilities is no surprise to most ELA teachers, as we are used to hearing from prominent writers about the role that reading plays in their work. For example, during her speech accepting the 2014 Sandroff Lifetime Achievement Award from the National Book Critics Circle, Toni Morrison said, "Writing for me is just a very sustained process of reading" (Morrison, 2015). Conversely, Stephen King (2000) wrote, "The real importance of reading is that it creates an ease and intimacy with the process of writing" (p. 150).

Scholastic recently released an entire collection of essays from writers on the impact of reading. In it, humorist Roy Blount, Jr. noted that, "[n]obody ever finishes learning to read" (2014, p. 121). Coretta Scott King Award winner and former National Teacher of the Year Sharon Draper wrote that when she got her library card, she "ran with joyful anticipation to the great adventure of reading the rest of the books in the library. I am still there" (2014, p. 166).

And perhaps the author who illustrated the clearest path from reader to writer was Pam Muñoz Ryan, who wrote:

> The act of reading and escaping into books allowed me to live many more lives than my real one. Books allowed me to travel beyond Bakersfield, California. They helped me put my world in perspective, especially when I did not fit in. I was comforted by

the characters' lives, living them vicariously, as I muddled through my own. [. . .] Later, all of those dots on the path—hearing family stories, the luxury of dramatic play, reading and loving books—eventually led me to my writing life and the most wonderful gift in return, readers. (2014, p. 163)

I'd imagine that most ELA teachers would nod their heads upon reading Ryan's words. We recognize the inherent connection between writing and reading, and we realize that each informs, complements, cooperates with, and inspires the other. However, so often our secondary ELA curricula continues to be segregated into reading units OR writing units. Sometimes, writing units are taught in complete isolation from the reading of genre-specific mentor texts. And, while I bet most ELA teachers would report having students write during reading units, I'd also wager that most (if not all) of this writing is for the purpose of literary analysis. Of course it's important for students to be able to articulate their thinking and learning through writing, and analytical writing can be useful to assess what students have learned from reading and discussing literature. However, I'd argue that there's no better way to help students master literary elements than by their writing with those elements.

As an alternative (or in addition) to a short answer test or a literary analysis essay, crafting a creative writing piece in the genre that you're studying and drawing from the reading texts in the unit as mentor texts is a potent reading assessment. Dorfman and Capelli (2007) wrote, "[m]entor texts serve as snapshots into the future. They help students envision the writer they can become" (p. 3). Even if finished creative pieces aren't groundbreaking in terms of quality, crafting plot, creating characters, and using literary elements will help students to internalize and gain greater ownership of the same, which, in turn, helps students to develop a more complex lens with which to analyze reading texts. Besides what's evident in their finished products, teachers can also gain insight into students' level of mastery through reading their writers' memos and conferencing with them one-on-one. Creative writing also adds some autonomy to reading assessment since, rather than answering the same literary analysis questions across the board, students can individualize and personalize their work.

In "Part I: Reading the Truth," I presented a sequence of activities for students to extensively read and analyze a narrative nonfiction text set. "Part II: Writing the Truth" presents the culminating assessment for the unit: writing a personal essay. Dorfman and Capelli (2007) wrote that:

young writers should be introduced first as readers. They need to hear and appreciate the story and characters as well as the rhythms, words, and message. Only then can they return to a well-loved book and examine it through the eyes of a writer. (p. 5)

Drawing from the techniques and elements they encountered during the reading portion of the unit, students will apply their learning by crafting their own contribution to the narrative nonfiction genre.

And, even though David Coleman and some administrators may disapprove, sharing thoughts and feelings through a personal essay has benefits in addition to serving as an effective reading assessment. In the Introduction, I briefly mentioned some of the reported positive psychological effects of personal writing, and I'll reference these again in Part II. Also, as the featured student work will hopefully demonstrate, the process of writing personal essays, especially while drawing from narrative nonfiction mentor texts, can help students discover a lot about themselves, other people, and the world. Furthermore, through the study of narrative nonfiction as outlined in this book, students come to realize that their stories are not inherently interesting to others unless they write them in an inherently interesting way.

In the syllabus for his creative nonfiction course, the late David Foster Wallace wrote:

In the grown-up world, creative nonfiction is not *expressive* writing but rather *communicative* writing. And an axiom of communicative writing is that the reader does not automatically care about you (the writer), nor does she find you fascinating as a person, nor does she feel a deep natural interest in the same things that interest you. (Foster Wallace, 2014, para. 7)

Wallace's quote doesn't initially sound too different from Coleman's, but there's one key difference. Rather than discouraging personal writing as did Coleman, Wallace encouraged a sense of critical self-awareness about which stories we share and how we share them. Writing a personal essay while keeping Wallace's advice in mind becomes more than self-centered navel gazing, but rather an essential step in students moving from a "me to we" mentality as they consider how their stories fit into the broader mosaic of humanity.

Chapter 4 includes activities to help students get started with the personal essay; Chapter 5 includes perspective on helping students to polish their essays and go deeper into the genre; and Chapter 6 includes wisdom from two successful narrative nonfiction writers: MK Asante (author of the best-selling memoir *Buck*) and Johanna Bear (a student writer who has earned national recognition for multiple nonfiction pieces).

Thankfully, several factors combined to preserve my department's reading of literature beyond Internet articles. First, my former department chair retired before he could successfully eliminate novels from our curriculum. His successor was the same chair who worked with me to bring *The Soloist* onto our tenth grade reading list, and she was appalled (appropriately, in my opinion) at the thought of eliminating actual books from English class. Second, while not perfect, the Common Core does restore more of a role for the narrative mode beyond fifth grade. In fact, the Common Core is surprisingly conducive to teaching this type of narrative nonfiction reading unit anchored by the writing of a personal essay. Appendix C includes a complete list of the CCSS reading and writing standards addressed in a unit that includes both reading *and* writing narrative nonfiction.

Chapter

Crafting the Truth:
Getting Started with Personal Essays

Student Snapshots

What did you learn about yourself by writing a personal essay?

"I learned that you should be willing to fight for who you are, and that a true sense of self requires constant questioning and change, especially for a teenager." Alex P.

"I learned that I have been independent, much more than I realized." Violet B.

What did you learn about others and/or the world by writing a personal essay?

"People aren't always who they say they are, but even a person everyone perceives as negative can change your life for the better." Rowan Y.

"People don't usually hurt you unless they are hurt themselves." Ellen D.

Which is harder to write—fiction or nonfiction? If you want to inspire a spirited debate among young writers, ask them this question. If your students follow the pattern that mine have demonstrated, I predict they'll fall into two camps; the first offering comments like "fiction is way harder because you have to make everything up, so the possibilities are endless!" and the other claiming "nonfiction is harder because you can't change what happened to make a better story."

The reality, of course, is that good writing is hard in any genre. There is no debate between fiction and nonfiction because effective storytelling contains the same core elements. Good stories are both true and compelling. "But the truth we seek from novels is different from the truth we seek from memoirs. Novels, you might say, represent 'a truth' about life, whereas memoirs and nonfiction accounts represent 'the truth' about specific things that have happened" (Mendelsohn, 2010, para. 24).

Stephen King (2000) wrote that "the job of fiction is to find the truth inside the story's web of lies" (p. 159). Even the most fantastically imagined fictional tales have to ring true on some level in order to connect with readers. King continued, "When the reader hears strong echoes of his or her own life and beliefs, he or she is apt to become more invested in the story" (p. 159). The challenge of fiction, then, is not just "to make stuff up" but rather to use the freedom of fictive invention to explore and reflect truth.

Narrative nonfiction has the opposite problem. Since, barring lapses in honesty or memory, the truth is already established in a nonfiction story, the craft is to present this truth in an interesting way. Phillip Lopate (2013) wrote, "The challenge faced by the nonfiction writer is to take something that actually happened, to herself or to others, and try to render it as honestly and compellingly as possible" (p. 13). In other words, an effective nonfiction storyteller needs to employ the plot and character techniques of fiction in order to make true stories most interesting.

Fiction and nonfiction storytelling, then, are two sides of the same coin. Good fiction reflects some truth about real life, and good nonfiction reads like fiction. My students usually have more practice telling stories through fiction, and most of their nonfiction writing has been in academic form. So, when I ask my students to write narrative nonfiction, they struggle not only with what to write about, but also with where to start.

In this chapter, I present four lessons, each with a number of corresponding activities, which help students to build confidence and momentum in writing narrative nonfiction. And, as they're developing concrete skills, they're also building a reservoir of ideas from which they can draw and write about. In my classes and workshops, I usually engage students in the activities first, and then I reveal the lesson. For the purpose of presenting them in this book, though, it makes sense to offer the lesson first, followed by the activities.

Students are more successful in choosing a topic and completing a draft of a personal essay if they do so after working through these lessons.

Lesson 1: Write your Truth

How many truths are there? This is another good one for discussion and debate. When I ask my tenth graders this question, some offer counter-questions like, "what do you mean by truth? How do you define that term?" Others confidently claim that there's only one truth, it exists independently of us, and we may or may not be aware of it. I like this answer, and I agree with it to some extent, but the nature of truth is not so simple.

Regarding relativity in quantum physics, Stephen Hawking (1996) wrote, "observers who are moving relative to each other will assign different times and positions to the same event. No particular observer's measurements are any more correct than any other observer's, but all the measurements are related" (p. 33). What Hawking suggested is that our perspective, though true in its own right, may differ from those of others who experienced the same event, and no one's perspectives are less true than others.

Gutkind (2012) connected this idea to narrative nonfiction:

Truth is personal—it is what we see, assume, and believe, filtered through our own lens and orientation. Although it may revolve around the same subject or issue, the truth as one person perceives it may not be the same truth another person sees. . . . There are many truths to a story and many versions of the same story. (p. 19)

Gutkind and Hawking suggest that there is a dual nature to truth. There is the relative truth, which is based on our individual perspectives of any given event, and then there is the ultimate truth, which exists independently of any individual and encompasses each of these relative truths. In narrative nonfiction, we can't tell the "whole truth" since we can't possibly know every other perspective. Instead, we offer our piece of the truth. By doing so, and by reading the relative truths of others, we come closer to understanding the complex nature of universal truth, which is that different people experience the same things differently.

In order to help students work with the concept of writing their truth, I engage them in an activity called the "Perspective Walk."

Activity: Perspective Walk

Without explaining the purpose, take students on a 5–10 minute walk around campus. If it's nice and you are able, take them outside. Lead them up and down stairs, if possible. If they're not being disruptive, let them drift and spread out as you go. Engage them in conversation, but when they ask where you are taking them, or why you're walking, be purposefully evasive.

When you return to the classroom, ask students to write the story of your walk. Tell them to include any notable conversations or events and to make it as active as possible. Give them about 10 minutes to write, and since they can't tell the whole story in that time frame, encourage them to focus on the most notable parts of the walk. As students are working, I also write my own story of our walk and focus on my observations of student behavior along with my inner monologue.

When students have finished writing, have them pair-share first, and then ask for a few volunteers to read their scenes to the class. Once the class has heard several perspectives (and perhaps yours as well), reveal Lesson 1 as "Write your Truth" and engage students in discussion on the concepts of relative versus ultimate truth and the role of relative truth in narrative nonfiction.

If you're unable to take your students out of the classroom, any shared experience that includes some individual variety will do. You could substitute a walk for a quick classroom game or a random demonstration or quick creative exercise. I find the activity works best when students don't have any hints about the lesson. Since students respond differently to surprises, their varying reactions lend themselves well to the activity.

After my students pair-share their responses, I usually ask them the "how many truths are there?" question. Then, I share my story of the walk and invite several students to read theirs as well. Once we've considered various perspectives on the same event, I show them the Figure 4.1 Perspective Chart, and we talk about how sharing our relative truths and considering those of others help to give us a better understanding of ultimate truth.

Figure 4.2 includes excerpts from several student responses along with my own after a recent Perspective Walk.

Figure 4.1 Perspective Chart

Figure 4.2 Differing Student Accounts of a Shared Event

The Story of Our Walk: Relative Truths from Period 2
Mr. G:
"Oh my Gosh. I can't believe you! Here, Mr. G, I found this phone! Where are we going? This is just for exercise. Are you throwing us a surprise party? Can we just walk all class?"
The shouts overlapped and blended in with each other. Before I could focus on one comment, the next had eclipsed it. If I told them the size of the headache I woke up with this morning, would they stop? Would they even hear? If I chastised them like a kindergarten class for disrupting other students, would they be ashamed, or would they just snicker?
Clang, Clang, Clang. My reverie was interrupted by Bart repeatedly clanging the book drop as a student jumped on another's back. "Here comes the librarian," I thought, remembering another time when my students were returning a book, and the librarian had come out to scold them, thinking they were just causing trouble at the book drop.
Jenna:
Mr. Griffith announces to the class that it is time to go to the library to drop off our books. Hayden and I walk down together arm in arm, singing songs from Pocahontas. We arrive outside of the library, and I suddenly forget my task. I catch Bart at the corner of my eye and see that he puts his book in the book return. I stack mine on top and Bart yells over the group of people to try fitting as many books as possible into the small book return.
Our class continues walking down the hall, down the stairs, and across again to head back to the classroom. Bart begins to talk nonsense, jumbling his sentences, and we take note of the Herd 100 quilt and talk of our experiences creating it. We continue down the hall and into the last set of doors, and Bart begins to sprint up the stairs. Not amused, I walk moderately next to Sophie. We reach the top and Bart shouts "Ha! Beat you!"
Bart:
Tyler put his book in the book return, and I slammed it shut on his hand.
"Owww . . . Bart!" Tyler cried out.
"Oops. Sorry. I didn't know your hand was in there, honestly." I replied quickly. Tyler still moaned with pain because he is weak.
As our small group traveled down the hall, I walked with Ally, who speculated, "I bet we're going to see Mr. G's old swimming trophies."
Ally:
I severely questioned why we were walking in circles because my legs were beginning to hurt, and then I saw Hayden, Kyle, and SJ trying to jump up and touch the flags on the bridge. Kyle was the only one to touch the banister, and I decided to show him up. I come down from my miraculous jump, and SJ takes my phone. I put her in a headlock to get it back, and it drops to the floor.
"Is your phone ok?" SJ asks.
"No." I respond as I sprint up the stairs and into our class. I still wonder the reason for our journey.
Tyler:
Not wanting my book destroyed, I wait to place mine in until Bart lets the first group of books fall down in. As my hand is innocently placing my book into the metal chute, Bart slams it shut,

crushing my hand for a brief moment. It smarts quite a bit, my fingers red and swollen, but all I can do is stare at Bart with a look of shock and confusion. *Did he not see my hand still there?* We continue on our way back to the classroom, but Mr. Griffith takes us on a different path than the one on which we traveled first. Bewildered, we follow. I walk beside Reghan, Kristen and Ally, talking about how I didn't get hired at the ice cream parlor The Meadows. Reghan says she feels bad about it, so we start to think of a fool-proof plan to get me hired.

Mackenzie:

We left the English classroom, filing out of the door in clumps and scattering into the hallway. We walked towards the library, small conversations forming as we made our way across the walking bridge that connected the buildings. As we approached the library doors, we remembered that there was a drop box in the hallway. We decided to try shoving as many books in as we could before closing it and sending them into the hole.

By learning that their relative truths are important and valuable, students must also consider that the relative truths of others, even if they're different, are also important. This is why people can't get enough of true life stories revolving around huge events of shared consciousness like 9/11 or World War II; there are so many perspectives to share. The potency of relative truth is revealed by such works as John Hersey's (1946) *Hiroshima*, which recounts the stories of six civilian survivors living in the aftermath of the atomic bomb. Adding the six unique stories from Hersey's narrative nonfiction novel to what we've already heard about the Enola Gay and the Manhattan project gives us a more sobering and comprehensive truth regarding a complex historical event.

Considering such powerful examples prompts the next challenge and the next lesson in response to a likely next question: "What should I write about?"

Lesson 2: Build the Reservoir

"But I'm just not that exciting! Nothing ever happens to me. I don't go anywhere. I don't know anyone who's interesting. Who would want to read about me?" My students commonly give me these types of questions, comments, complaints, and excuses when I tell them we're writing personal essays. Some of these are the typical gibes and jeers that accompany the announcement of any assignment involving effort, but they also possibly reveal something more humbling. Though students may post frivolously on social media, or jabber about themselves in person, when they're asked to write something personal and of significance, many lack the confidence.

When push comes to shove, they don't see themselves as exceptional or interesting.

I've heard that it's a cliché among undergraduate creative nonfiction instructors that they get a lot of "dead grandma" essays. This may seem callous, but these instructors have gathered that the worst and most significant event in many young creative writers' lives is the loss of a grandparent. A conclusion here would be that young writers lack the life experience to write important or compelling nonfiction. I disagree.

First, I've had teenage essayists write about incredibly honest, brave, and revelatory topics. One student, who was not out to his classmates, wrote about coming out to his parents and how they hadn't yet accepted the news. I had a student write about her mom kicking her out of the house after she got pregnant and had an abortion, while another student wrote about how an anti-abortion rally was a life-changing experience. One student wrote about his parents' successful fly-by-night escape and rendezvous in the wake of the Bosnian genocide. I've had students write about suicide attempts, being homeless, and their parents' struggles with drugs and alcohol. I even had a student make an effective play off of the dead grandma cliché by sharing how she had to attend her grandmother's funeral on her own birthday.

Many students have had amazing life experiences that would stack up against the range of interesting subjects found in any grown-up essay collection. However, a lot of writers (both student and adult) don't have fantastic experiences to draw from. The good news is that there's a lot of great nonfiction writing about mundane, everyday, relatable topics. Subjects like love and loss, personal triumphs and failures, pet peeves and compulsions, fears and confessions, etc. are universal and can be of interest to a broad audience, if they're well written.

Lesson 2: "Build the Reservoir" is intended to help students identify and capture a wide range of experiences and subjects before they are asked to choose something to write about. As Ray Bradbury (1990) noted, "[s]ometimes . . . ideas come when you're not ready to follow up on them. Good ideas are rare" (p. 77). We can provide methods, however, that students can use to capture and store their good ideas when they come. As Bradbury recommended, "jot down incidents and ideas for the future so that you'll always have another story to tell."

The first activity for this lesson also comes from Bradbury and is one that many of us use weekly when we visit the grocery store: make a list.

Activity: Listing

This one is pretty simple. Ask students to make lots of lists on lots of different topics in their notebooks or in a folder on their computers. If your students keep a writer's notebook throughout the year, ask them to make a different list each week or twice a month. If your students don't keep writers' notebooks, then ask them to make a variety of lists over the course of a week or two. I usually ask students to make one list in class and another one for homework each day for a week. The purpose of these lists is to take advantage of a few moments of creative free association and add to a creative reservoir from which they can draw ideas later. Lists also give a space that writers can return to when they think of items to add.

Lists can be on anything, but I'd encourage assigning ones that generate good stories. You can also have students invent lists on topics of their own choosing. Here are a few of my favorite lists to assign:

Make a list of . . .

- ◆ The most interesting people you know or have met (remember that interesting doesn't have to be in a good way).
  - ● Next to the list of interesting people, make a corresponding list of the qualities and characteristics that make them interesting.
- ◆ The stories you find yourself telling over and over.
- ◆ The experiences that have had the biggest impact on your life.
- ◆ Experiences that haunt you.
- ◆ Your personal triumphs.
- ◆ First times.
- ◆ Favorites and least favorites.
- ◆ Pet peeves.
- ◆ Most embarrassing moments.
- ◆ Best and worst things others have said to you.

After students have developed several lists, ask them to go back through and put checkmarks next to the items that would be of interest to readers who don't know them. When students consider which of their stories would appeal to a broader audience than their family or friends, they start to zero in on the best possibilities for personal essays. If lists aren't too private and students are comfortable, they can also trade with partners and have partners identify the list items that are most interesting.

According to *Zen in the Art of Writing* (1990), Bradbury kept all sorts of lists: lists of titles, lists of nouns, lists of people he'd like to put on Mars. He wrote that "[t]hese lists were the provocations, finally, that caused my better stuff to surface. I was feeling my way toward something honest, hidden under the trapdoor at the top of my skull" (p. 17). Bradbury's list items were the conscious peaks of richer ideas that lived in his subconscious. After making his lists, he'd see patterns that would comprise his best stories. Figure 4.3 includes photographs of three student lists.

The first includes a list of memorable characters and their corresponding characteristics, and the second and third are lists of impactful life events (the events that are starred are the ones the students have identified to have appeal to an audience beyond their friends and family).

Recently, I was considering how social media posts are sort of mini-personal essays and that one of the values of writing narrative nonfiction is the focused and detailed exploration and reflection on significant life events. This idea led me to consider a new type of listing activity that might help students identify moments worth writing about.

Figure 4.3 Sample Student Lists

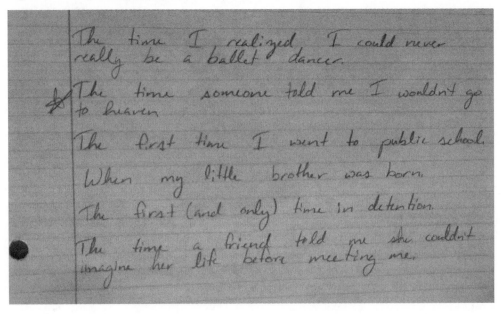

The time I...

- Caroline and I were hanging out and Caroline randomly said she was pregnant

✓ - My grandma almost got shot by a gang

✓ - sliced my leg open from my knee to my hip with a stick
- when I got an F on a 5th grade quiz
✓ - got separated from my family by getting on the wrong subway in NYC

- become friends the host at a restaurant in NYC

- when I hurt my knee at Nerd Camp
Events that have a large impact on my life

my grandfather (████)	Self absorbed, overbearing, smokes a pipe, insensitive, oblivious, intelligent
Meghan	Bitter, judgemental, athletic assumes the world is out to get her
Geo	Enthusiastic, crazy, funny, kind

Activity: Mining Social Media

As a homework assignment, ask students to go into the social media accounts they use most frequently and review their posts, tweets, photos, tags, etc. from the last few weeks, months, or the past year (depending on how frequently they post). Ask students to ignore the posts that were silly, frivolous, or no longer relevant, but to list the posts which have a bigger story to tell, especially stories that stand the test of time and that may be of interest to others. Which are the posts where there is still something to be learned, discovered, or understood?

Whether it's through Instagram, Twitter, Pinterest, Facebook, Tumblr, or a similar platform (or combination of platforms), many students are keeping meticulous electronic diaries in the form of their tweets, tags, posts, photos, shares, etc. While many of their posts may be silly, frivolous, or cryptic to anyone other than the poster, students can review these posts to remind themselves of some of the most significant moments in their lives and those that might bear further examination through a personal essay. After recently asking students to mine their social media, one of my tenth graders jokingly told me, "I spent an hour looking back at everything I've posted over the past year, and I've decided to rethink my life."

For narrative nonfiction, especially, one of the best follow-up activities to listing is to ask students to choose one of their list items as a prompt for further writing. Daily or weekly prompts are another common and effective activity to use for building a creative reservoir.

Activity: Responding to Prompts

Ask students to regularly respond to creative prompts in low-risk free-writes. I usually choose five prompts at a time (students can always invent their own as an alternative, if they don't get any ideas from my selections) and ask students to choose one and write for 10 minutes, focusing on creating an active scene.

Teachers can get creative writing prompts from many places (or invent their own), but one book that I enjoy using is *642 Things to Write About* (2011) published by the San Francisco Writers Grotto. While this book doesn't include prompts specific to nonfiction, teachers can easily choose ones that lend themselves well to true accounts, such as:

◆ Something you had that was stolen.
◆ Tell the true story of a dramatic moment in your life, but weave in one secret and one lie.
◆ Open your kitchen cabinet. Write a scene incorporating the first three things you see.
◆ The road to hell is paved with good intentions.
◆ A conversation that you weren't supposed to overhear.

There's also a *642 Things to Write About* (826 Valencia, 2014) Young Writer's Edition, which includes prompts more suited to younger writers, like:

◆ Write about something you hate to love.
◆ Write a guidebook about a place you've been to only in stories. It could be a place that your parents talk about all the time or the setting of your favorite book.
◆ What's the funniest thing about someone you love?
◆ Write about the first time you heard your favorite song.
◆ What is something you wish someone had told you about being a kid?

After students have completed their prompt, ask them to partner up to pair-share and then allow several volunteers to read their responses aloud to the class.

While daily or weekly prompts are already a fairly typical activity in many English classes, it's important that students understand the purpose of the activity; to generate ideas that might be returned to later. It's okay if a prompt on any given day doesn't reap quality writing; then, it's just creative practice for building writing stamina. But, all it takes is the right prompt at the right moment for a student to get the perfect idea for a longer piece.

I tend not to grade these low-risk, high-frequency prompts. As Kittle (2008) wrote, "[q]uick writing is play. This is something most students crave: to write freely, to experiment with their thinking and ideas, to try on voice, or to rant about life. No grades attached: It is a time to speak" (p. 27). Encouraging students to play and experiment in their writing without the potential consequence or prescriptiveness of a grade can help them to identify and develop better ideas.

Daily or weekly prompts can also be used as an exercise for developing one of the key skills in writing narrative nonfiction: writing in scenes.

Lesson 3: Put the Reader in Your Shoes

"Show, don't tell." This is one of the most common and frequently repeated maxims of creative writing instruction. Still, it's another one that's easier said than done, especially when we ask students to *tell* a story rather than *show* a story. Especially in personal writing, we often resort to sharing how we felt in a given moment. Most of us start by recounting details passively in order to share them with others. But, the best storytellers reconstruct rather than recount. They make us feel their situational emotions rather than just making sure we understand how they felt. Engaging the audience in this way is essential to compelling narrative nonfiction, and writing in scenes is an effective way to do it. "Writing in scenes represents the difference between showing and telling" (Gutkind, 2012, p. 106).

Gutkind (2012) wrote, "[s]cenes are the building blocks of creative nonfiction, the foundation and anchoring elements of what we do" (p. 105), and the easiest way to get secondary students to consider what constitutes a scene is to ask them about the elements of a film or play scene. Chances are they'll come up with some of the same components that Gutkind mentioned; "[f]irst, a scene must contain action. Something happens" (p. 114) and, "scenes have a start and a finish, a beginning and an end" (p. 119). When students are able to use active scenes in their writing, it allows the reader to experience the story from the writer's perspective rather than just hearing about it second-hand.

In order to encourage students to write in scenes, I ask them to return to their lists and prompts.

Activity: Scene-Writing

Ask students to incorporate items from their lists into brief, active scenes that include action and dialogue and have a clear beginning and ending. I have found one of the most effective lists to start with is the list of the most memorable people students have encountered along with a corresponding list of the characteristics that made those people memorable.

Ask students to:

◆ Choose one of the memorable people from your list. Bring one of their memorable characteristics to life in a brief, active scene. In other words, use action and dialogue to show the character demonstrating the characteristic.

As a test, when students pair-share, ask the listening partner to identify the characteristic that he or she picked up on from the scene.

You can also apply scene-writing in other ways by asking students to incorporate other list items into scenes or to respond to certain prompts with active scenes.

For example:

◆ Choose a post or photograph from your social media mining list. Write a brief and active scene to show the story behind the post or photograph.

With effective scene-writing practice, student writers start to make purposeful decisions for including certain scenes. Rather than just saying, "Here's what happened," they consider, "what do I want to use this scene to show? What will these actions and dialogue demonstrate?" They use the scene as a tool for engaging readers and embedding information. As Gutkind (2012) noted, "a good real-life scene can show readers an aspect of character and personality that a writer could never achieve by telling it" (p. 113).

Figure 4.4 includes photographs of scenes from two student-writers' notebooks.

In the first, a student attempts to show the manipulative, hateful, and "judgy" nature of one of her seventh grade teachers; and in the second, the scene shows an unpredictable, self-absorbed, talented, and impulsive ballet instructor at work.

Once students have considered perspective and relative truth, started to build a creative reservoir of ideas, and worked with the scene as a building block for a longer piece, the next lesson is how to weave it all together.

Figure 4.4 Sample Student Scenes Generated from Lists

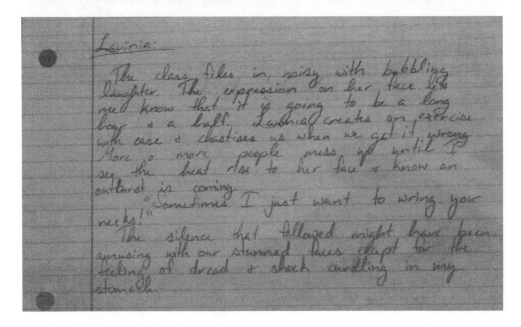

Lesson 4: Frame it Right

After identifying potential topics and working with some of the key elements of narrative nonfiction, the next question many student writers need to answer is, "where do I start?" People often say that first impressions are paramount, and the same is true for the opening lines of stories and personal essays. Stephen King was quoted in an interview with *The Atlantic* as suggesting that, "an opening line should invite the reader to begin the story. It should say: Listen. Come in here. You want to know about this" (Fassler, 2013).

But often, when students are considering how to begin their personal essays, teachers respond with a smattering of options: "You can start with a quote, a rhetorical question, dialogue, action, an interesting statistic," etc. While each of these techniques may be effective in its own right, crafting an effective opening takes more consideration than simply selecting from a menu. In the *Atlantic* interview, King asked, "[h]ow can a writer extend an appealing invitation—one that's difficult, even, to refuse?" (Fassler, 2013). In order to help my students answer this question, I like to engage them in an evaluation exercise using actual titles and first lines from published essays.

Activity: Evaluating First-lines

Select opening lines from ten published personal essays. You may pull these from a variety of sources including print or online anthologies or creative writing journals. One of my favorite texts to use for this activity is the yearly *Best American Essays* series, edited by Robert Atwan along with a different guest editor each year. While any of these collections would do, I particularly like to use *The Best American Essays 2013*, which were guest edited by Cheryl Strayed (Strayed, 2013). This edition, more than others I've used, has a good variety of interesting openings.

Once you've selected ten opening lines, read the title of the essay followed by the opening line and ask students to evaluate how interested they are on a scale of 1–5 (1 being least interested and 5 being most). Read each title/first line twice and ask students to record their initial number plus any comments to remind themselves why they chose that number. Once you've read and scored all ten, go back through them one at a time and discuss their scores.

There will likely be some variance in how students score each opening, so try to get a comment or two from folks who like the opening and from ones who don't. Then, read the rest of the opening paragraph (or opening few paragraphs) and ask students to give a thumbs-up or thumbs-down as to whether their interest increased or decreased, followed by a few comments about what influenced the second rating.

Here are two openings that I particularly like from *The Best American Essays 2013* (Strayed, 2013):

◆ From Vanessa Veselka's "Highway of Lost Girls"

"In the summer of 1985, somewhere near Martinsburg, Pennsylvania, the body of a young woman was pulled from a truck-stop dumpster. I had just hitched a ride and was sitting in a nearby truck waiting for the driver to pay for gas so we could leave."

◆ From Kevin Sampsell's "I'm Jumping Off the Bridge"

"People usually just ask me where the bathroom is or if we are hiring. Sometimes they ask where they can find the latest Dan Brown novel or 'that book they just talked about on NPR.' On this day in late 2007, however, while I worked at the front info desk at Powell's Books in Portland Oregon, a frazzled-looking young guy stood silently in front of me."

By evaluating actual essay openings through this first-lines activity, students get a sense of the kinds of beginning that are most captivating to them rather than just choosing an approach randomly. Since all of the essays in an anthology have already been curated and juried by editors, this activity proves that, even with "good" published writing, the reader still retains judgment based on his or her own tastes. Students also get the sense that many of the options they've been presented with in the past (like rhetorical question, interesting statistics, etc.) aren't used that often by real writers. While opening lines are very important, most writers start with a simple variation of "here's the deal . . ."

The opposite book-end of a personal essay, the closing lines, are also important. The memoirist Jane Bernstein said at the 2014 *Creative Nonfiction* magazine conference in Pittsburgh that the unwritten last line of any personal essay or memoir should be "and nothing was the same after that" (Bernstein, 2014). When I present this quote to students, some of them think that it means that personal essays have to be about an earth-shattering event but, as we discussed previously, some great nonfiction writing is about simple shifts in perspective. To help students understand those

Figure 4.5 Four Lessons for Writing Engaging Nonfiction

From Me to We:
Four Lessons for Writing Engaging Nonfiction

Lesson 1: Write Your Truth

- Activity: Perspective Walk- Take students on a 5-10 minute walk around campus without explaining the purpose. When you return, have students write the story of their walk. Have students share and use the variance in the accounts to demonstrate the difference between relative and ultimate truth.

Lesson 2: Build the Reservoir

- Activities: Over a period of time, have students make lists, write to prompts, keep writers' notebooks, and mine social media posts so that they have plenty of ideas to draw from for an engaging personal essay.

- Example: Make a T-Chart List. On the left, list five of the most interesting people you've ever met. On the right, list the characteristics which make those people so interesting.

Lesson 3: Put the Reader in Your Shoes

- Activity: Write in active scenes. Just like movie scenes, narrative scenes have a beginning and an end, and something happens in between. Use action, dialogue and active verbs to show rather than tell.

- Example: Choose an interesting person from your list. Write a brief, active scene which shows that person demonstrating one of his/her interesting characteristics.

Lesson 4: Frame it Right

- Activity: Evaluating First-lines- To help students consider the power of first lines, choose an anthology (like the Best American Essays), read some actual opening lines to students and have them rank their interest from 1-5. After they've explained why, read the rest of the opening paragraph and have them give a thumbs up or a thumbs down as to whether their interest increased or decreased.

- And remember Jane Bernstein's suggested advice for an unspoken last line: "And nothing was the same after that." If students can put that at the end of a personal essay, they're done.

possibilities, I like to include a variation on Bernstein's quote: "I couldn't ever see things the same way after that."

While it doesn't make sense to craft ending lines until students have completed a pretty good draft of their story, considering Bernstein's quote and its variation helps students to know when they've arrived at a conclusive moment in the essay. And, after working with opening and closing lines, students just need to work with the middle.

"Scenes require some sort of order. One scene must follow another in a logical progression or pattern. That pattern, a story in itself, is called a frame" (Gutkind, 2012, p. 218). Students need to consider in which order they will present their related scenes and explanation to reflect on personal experience and connect with readers. Newkirk (2014) wrote, "[w]e are biologically predisposed to process experience though the lens of antecedents and consequences" (p. 24). Once students have drawn us in with a compelling opening and crafted some engaging scenes, they need to consider a logical cause and effect progression in order to help us connect to and understand their experiences and reflection.

Stepping students through the activities involved in these four lessons (write your truth, build the reservoir, put the reader in your shoes, and frame it right),ensures that they are in a much more confident position to successfully begin drafting a personal essay that's both meaningful for the writer and compelling for the reader.

Chapter

5

Polishing the Truth:
Digging Deeper into Personal Essays

Student Snapshots

What did you learn about yourself by writing a personal essay?

"I don't value family enough, I trust too easily, and sometimes kids are stronger than adults." Abby R.

"I learned that circumstances I go through affect and teach the people who love and care about me." Grace W.

What did you learn about others and/or the world by writing a personal essay?

"Environment has more of an impact on some people versus others. Not everyone is limited or unlimited by where they come from." Ian P.

"The world is full of adventure and amazing experiences waiting to happen—you just have to be willing to explore and take some hikes." Kristen L.

"Should I actually say, I mean, write the word?" My students had completed the sequence of activities presented in Chapter 4, and now they were working individually to develop and polish their personal essay drafts. One student consulted me with a dilemma. She had chosen to tell a story about her grandparents. After their respective retirements, my student's grandfather tried to rope her grandmother into participating in his fleeting and fickle interests by buying her an increasingly random set of presents related to those hobbies (which she had no interest in herself). My student revealed a sequence of these gifts through holiday and birthday scenes before she arrived at the climax: Grandpa gives grandma a full beekeeping suit to which the surprised and frustrated grandma "drops the F-bomb" in front of an entire gathering of family (including the author). My student's dilemma was whether or not she could or should "drop the F-bomb" in her own essay.

We'll return to this anecdote in a moment. The purpose of this chapter, "Polishing the Truth," is to provide perspective on several topics related to students individually developing and finishing their personal essays. I didn't teach this unit based on a full workshop model, but after working through the sequence of activities from Chapter 4 as a class, I found it most useful to give students time to work as I conferenced with them individually and led brief mini-lessons addressing common needs as necessary. For each of the four major lessons from Chapter 4, I devoted one 50-minute class period each (four total) and, after that time, most students had selected an idea to write about. For the next workshopping phase, I also gave three or four class periods to work individually and conference with me. I realize that tight curricular calendars may not allow all teachers to budget so much time to writing a personal essay, and deadlines have to be imposed to some extent. But, in order to access their best work, it's important that students have at least some time to let their individual creative processes unfold naturally.

Here are my thoughts on some of the common issues and concerns that came up as my students workshopped their personal essays.

On the Use of Profanity

Returning to the opening anecdote, my student's dilemma was whether or not to drop the F-bomb in her personal essay. School rules compounded the issue since being reported for dropping the F-bomb resulted in an automatic suspension (which comically varied in our student handbook based on the part of speech. "F-you" earned a 3-day suspension since another person was the recipient of the profanity, whereas "I don't give an F" only earned 1 day out, since it was general profanity). The author did not typically disregard school rules, so she was cautious.

A recording engineer once warned the songwriter and poet Leonard Cohen that he should skip reading any "dirty" words during their recording, to which Cohen replied, "There are no dirty words. Ever" (NFB, 2014). Cohen's brief and dismissive response raises the issue of context with regards to profanity.

Stephen King (2000) elaborated:

> My mother, God rest her, didn't approve of profanity or any such talk; she called it "the language of the ignorant." This did not, however, keep her from yelling "Oh Shit!" if she burned the roast or nailed her thumb a good one while hammering a picture-hook in the wall. Nor does it preclude most people, Christian as well as heathen, from saying something similar (or even stronger) when the dog barfs on the shag carpet or the car slips off the jack. It's important to tell the truth; so much depends on it. (p. 186)

My student's first draft tried, unsuccessfully, to capture the comic shock of her grandma dropping the F-bomb without actually using the word. For the sake of the piece, she had to include it, and she looked to me for permission to do so. While some teachers may balk at allowing profanity in student writing, it's important to recognize the difference between gratuitous and strategic profanity, especially in creative work. There's a difference between a student shouting curses in the middle of class and a student including accurate dialogue in writing, especially if that dialogue is essential to the story. While I don't necessarily encourage students to use profanity in their writing, I do encourage them to accurately recreate their memory of characters' dialogue. If that dialogue is essential to the story, it's important to include it in its unspoiled entirety. Considering what rhetorical effect profanity will have and whether or not it's necessary is important for all writers, especially young ones. And, while some may suggest that students will jump to include profanity in their writing if restrictions are lifted, I've actually found that most err on the side of caution and only indulge when individually invited to do so.

However, I know that school rules and comfort level may prevent teachers from being as permitting as they'd like, which brings up the broader point of censorship, in general.

On Censorship

In general, I strongly believe that it's important not to censor young writers. Restrictions not only prevent writers from reaping the full breadth of psychological benefits that writing about personal experience provides, but they also prevent the best quality writing. When students are empowered to tell the stories they need to tell in the way that works best, they produce amazing work. Some recent topics that my tenth grade students chose to write about include reflecting on the birth of a brother who's 10 years younger, hiding from a blind man in a public restroom, witnessing the emergence of a sister's clinical depression, revealing a same-sex crush, finding a pet dog frozen to death after a snowstorm, learning about a grandfather's suicide via carbon monoxide, mourning the death of an uncle from a heart attack, being homeless, being obsessive compulsive, having a father disown the author, using cutting to manage anxiety, and living with the pain of ovarian cysts.

Obviously, this list showcases sensitive ground that students might not have elected to cover if either they didn't trust me or they were censored. If we ask them to, and they trust us, students will write bravely. But, sometimes, our intersecting roles as teacher require some form of censorship or at least a warning of consequence. For example, our role as mandatory reporter dictates that we must report signs of abuse. If a student raises concerns of self-harm or violence toward others, we're morally and legally obligated to intervene. The same holds true if students use a personal essay to confess crime or illicit activity. While the best narrative nonfiction is often the most honest and least censored, sometimes our consecutive duties as teacher require limitations not levied on adult writers outside of a school context.

In order to maintain a bond of trust with our students and to engender the best conditions for successful writing, if we must censor, we should clearly explain why we are censoring and what specific situations require limitation or have consequence. And, we should offer these disclaimers before students start writing.

On Peer-Review and Public Sharing

Kittle (2014) noted that writing the memoir or personal narrative has traditionally been the "unit you toss into September to get to know students before you actually begin teaching 'real' writing" (p. 4). It might be tempting to use personal writing as a get-to-know-you activity, but if that's the only place where students are engaging in personal writing, students likely aren't going to reveal the same vulnerability and honesty in their writing as they would after getting to know their teacher and classmates. I'd guess that the list of student topics I shared would be quite different had I taught the unit at the beginning of the school year rather than closer to the end. Trusting the class-room community is a key component to students being able to select from their full range of experiences, including the vulnerable ones, to write about.

Trust and vulnerability lead to the next important topic: the role of peer-review and public sharing. For any writer, the "going public" phase offers some trepidation. Once we've released our writing into the world, we have no control over how (or even if) readers react to it. Such trepidation is exacerbated by writing about true and personal events and people. So, my simple rule with regards to peer revision and public sharing is to always give students an out. Let students choose whether or not they're willing to trade their drafts with classmates, and allow them to select their partners if there are certain friends they're more comfortable with. Don't force public sharing.

Pennebaker and Evans (2014) presented evidence that expressive writ-ing can bring about positive biological effects including: increased immune function and signs of stress reduction; psychological benefits like improved long-term mood changes; and, behavioral changes revolving around being more productive both at work and socially. The additional good news is that, "[e]xpressive writing doesn't need to be read by anyone in order for you to benefit from it" (p. 17). Wilson (2011) presented two conditions that must be satisfied in order for expressive writing to generate such benefit: "people gain some distance from the event, so that thinking about it doesn't overwhelm them, and they analyze why the event occurred" (p. 57).

I typically encourage students, if they are willing, to trade their per-sonal essay drafts with multiple peer review partners, including ones they wouldn't normally work with, because this workshop model is the best chance writers have to glimpse how a variety of readers will react to their work before they release it. However, I also work to create a classroom atmosphere where students can elect to work as a quiet pair or individu-ally and apart from the rest of the group. Even if students only choose to share their personal essays with me, I can still assess the reading elements (as I outlined in the Interlude), and students can still benefit personally as Wilson and Pennebaker and Evans described.

On Dialogue

One of the most interesting techniques in both fiction and nonfiction story-telling, one of the best ways to add action, and one of the most effective ways to "show" (rather than tell) information is to include dialogue.

King (2000) said:

> It's dialogue that gives your cast their voices, and is crucial in defining their characters—only what people do tells us more about what they're like, and talk is sneaky: what people say often conveys their character to others in ways of which they—the speakers—are completely unaware. (p. 180)

While both fiction and nonfiction storytellers have to work to make their dialogue "sound" realistic, narrative nonfiction writers have the added responsibility of veracity. And being truthful can be difficult since it is near impossible, without the aid of a recording device, to remember exactly what was said during a conversation.

Most books on creative nonfiction recognize this limitation, and allowances are often made for the sake of plot and readers' interest. As long as writers aren't completely fabricating conversations that didn't happen or lying about what other people said, readers recognize that nonfiction story writers are reconstructing dialogue, to some extent. "The idea is to replicate the conversation vividly and to mirror memory and speculation with trust and good judgment" (Gutkind, 2012, p. 37). The important thing is that readers understand what moves the writer is making, and if any liberties are taken with regards to dialogue, there's some cue to indicate it.

To practice writing natural sounding dialogue, I encourage students to listen to their friends' conversations at lunch or during a study hall and practice writing them down. Alternatively, if they have access to friends or family members who are featured in their personal essays, they can practice listening to those folks talk and try to translate that into writing to get a feel for how they speak.

Another issue warranting a quick note or mini-lesson is the use of dialogue tags. In my experience students tend to want to use over-enthusiastic verbs paired with adverbs ("Jason exclaimed enthusiastically"), probably because they were encouraged somewhere along the way to "use something other than *said*." The only problem with this advice is that it's contrary to what's found in most celebrated writing.

Take a look at some of your curricular novels, and flip through to scan the dialogue, and chances are that you'll see "said" more than any other tag and minus additional descriptors at that.

An article on Scribophile explained:

> Consensus among professional editors and authors is that speech tags should be invisible in the prose so they don't distract or detract from story. Invisible dialogue tags use simple verbs. It's generally accepted and recommended that two verbs are preferred: *said* and *asked*. (Johnson, n.d., para. 5)

Once this new advice is offered to students, I find they are pretty effective at making their dialogue tags less apparent (which, in turn, helps readers get sucked into the conversation).

On the Role of Research in Creative Nonfiction

Also, the author's memory is not the only resource available for writing narrative nonfiction. It's a fallacy to discredit the narrative nonfiction genre as being just a biased, singular account. While it's true that some experiences are relative, as we explored with the perspective chart in Figure 4.1 and the related perspective walk activity, there are also many sources of information available to the nonfiction writer with which to verify details.

Such sources include photographs from the event or from the people and time period represented in the stories. Interviews with the key characters, if they're still living, can also help to supplement and even correct a writer's own memory. Historical details and pop culture references including music and other allusions help to anchor a story in a particular place and time and can all be researched through traditional means like internet databases and searches for relevant webpages, magazines, and newspaper articles.

Notable examples of well-researched narrative nonfiction abounds. In Jacqueline Woodson's (2014) national book award winning memoir-in-verse *Brown Girl Dreaming*, she juxtaposed historical events that align with her own personal development. In his memoir, *Buck* (2013), MK Asante (whom I interview in Chapter 6) included rap lyrics from songs he listened to during the time periods he recreated in his book. He also quoted from letters his brother sent him from prison and even from entries from his mother's diary. Use of such artifacts lends credence to Asante's memory of and reaction to the events of his life.

I encourage students to do their own research in this manner to supplement their memories, verify key details, and add layers to their personal essays.

On Telling the Truth

Hopefully, this should go without saying by now, but it bears repeating to students that they should resist the temptation to fabricate details in order to make their stories more interesting. As I referenced briefly in Chapter 1, there is an increasing list of authors, politicians, and even news anchors who have been called out for fabricating all or parts of published stories, and while they may have gotten away with it for a while, the eventual damage to their reputations is often irreparable.

If you have class time to listen and discuss, there's a fantastic segment of the 180 Degrees episode of *This American Life* called "Seeing the Forrest through the Little Trees" (Blumberg et al., 2013) where the producers explored the strange true story of Forrest Carter who wrote a book he labeled as a memoir called *The Education of Little Tree*, in which he revealed lessons he learned from his Cherokee grandparents. According to the podcast, this book is still on curricular reading lists across the country. The only problem is that Forrest Carter was actually Asa Carter, a former speechwriter for notoriously racist Alabama governor George Wallace. Even after Forrest was exposed as a fraud through national press, his book continued to be shelved as "memoir" and even as "Native American" under booksellers' categories. When I've used this podcast with students, they're often fascinated by how extensive Carter's fraud was and remains (even after the author's death), and the podcast is a really interesting format to deliver the true story behind the lie.

Even if you tell the truth under your real name, it can still be problematic. I often share with students Suzy Lee Weiss's (2013) editorial in the *Wall Street Journal* titled "To (All) the Colleges that Rejected Me." As the title suggests, the author wrote a tongue-in-cheek rebuttal to a rejection letter from her dream school. Unfortunately, her intended humor and the national forum for her publication drew fire from peers and adults alike who labeled Weiss as spoiled and entitled. Notably, *The Huffington Post* published a reaction from then high school junior Sam Lyons (2013), titled

"Why Suzy Lee Weiss is Completely Wrong." Whether or not Weiss's piece was funny and/or true and whether Lyons' reaction was spot-on or an overreaction is subject to debate.

Sharing these articles and perspectives with students and returning to the questions of narrator likeability and its relationship to trustability (that we explored in Chapter 3) is an interesting and important conversation for students to have as they're finishing their personal essays. The bottom-line is that it's usually best to be honest and forthright. Then, if readers don't like you or your viewpoint, at least you have the truth on your side.

On Structure

After working through the lessons of Chapter 4, most students have a solid idea that they want to develop into a personal essay, and they also usually have a few scenes in mind to include. However, a common struggle is how they tie their scenes together overall with a coherent plot that includes both engaging story and moments of reflection.

If you can get away with reading it in class or distributing it to students, Lamott's (1994) "Shitty First Drafts" chapter from *Bird by Bird* is really useful because it gives them permission to just get everything down on the page first, regardless of quality, and then they can polish later. If you can't get away with distributing the chapter to students, you might be able to pull a few quotes in order to give them the gist.

For example, Lamott writes:

> Very few writers know what they're doing until they've done it. Nor do they go about their business feeling dewy and thrilled. They do not type a few stiff warm-up sentences and then find themselves bounding like huskies across the snow. (p. 93)

Lamott does an excellent job of reminding us that writing is work, and once we get a draft written, then we can move things around and shape them to be better.

Another excellent tool for teaching structure is Bernabei and Hall's (2012) "kernel essays" (p. 11), where the authors guide students into a simple sequence of moments with guiding questions such as: "Where were you? What happened first? What happened next? What happened last? What's one life lesson that this moment brought you?" Answering these questions in order provides a simple frame that students can flesh out with active scenes to populate a personal essay. Besides this beginning frame, Bernabei and Hall also offer an appendix with dozens of potential frames to help students structure personal essays including "Pet Peeve" (What you saw first, what you said to yourself, what else you saw, what you decided, what you know now), and "I Will Never" (I will never . . ., If I did . . ., This would cause . . ., I've seen it before like when . . ., So I have decided that . . ., I will probably change my mind if . . .) (p. 147). Though some writers might find these frames simplistic, they can be a great help to struggling writers in sequencing scenes.

Another useful tip is working towards what Early and DeCosta (2012) called the "so-what" moment. "[T]his was the part of the essay where, as writers, they needed to move back from the story and describe the lessons learned or the reason the story resonated in their lives" (pp. 50–51). Early and DeCosta particularly suggest this in the case of the college essay where the personal experience leads to some sort of lesson or revelation.

A final tip on structure is for a writer to simply show or share their evolving thought process surrounding an event or sequence of events. Newkirk (2005) called such framing "[e]arned insights" from "the speculation and the examination of experience that went into them" (p. 67). Students can lead their readers step by step through not only the key events in the plot of their stories but also the sequence of the development of their thoughts and reactions to those events. We respect these kinds of stories, and are moved by them, because we have had access to the process of their formulation.

On Teachers Writing with Students

Gallagher (2011) wrote, "If we want our students to grow as writers, we have to come out from behind the writing curtain and model to our students what good writers do" (p. 225). With narrative nonfiction, this statement grows even truer considering the vulnerability that we're asking students to demonstrate by writing about their lives, themselves, and the real people who have impacted them. Dorfman and Capelli (2007) noted that, "[a] teacher of writing must be a teacher who writes" (p. 8), which I agree with for several reasons. First, writing ourselves and sharing that writing with students demonstrates a willingness to be vulnerable in the same manner that we're asking of our students, which, in turn, builds trust. Also, writing our own personal essays (or whatever genre we're teaching) helps us stay in touch with how difficult and demanding the writing process can be.

When teachers demonstrate their thinking and writing processes to produce a piece in the specific genre that they're asking students to write in, it empowers students to do the same. "I don't provide 'answers' in class, I provide possibilities" (Kittle, 2008, p. 81). I share with students creative nonfiction pieces that I have had published, and I explain my purposes and processes in creating those. I also show them works in progress and share challenges I'm encountering in my current work. Perhaps most importantly, I share with them examples of the many rejection letters I've received after submitting my work for publication. My hope with this sharing is that, rather than simply seeing me as someone who makes them struggle by writing about themselves, they see me as a partner in that struggle, and one who believes in its greater rewards.

On Writing for Publication

Something I continue to struggle with is how to empower student writers to experiment and take risks when their personal essays serve as a unit assessment on which I will ultimately have to assign a grade. I have not yet completely answered the question of how to balance student empowerment and the imposition of a grade on complete creative empowerment, but I know that one component is encouraging students to consider polishing their pieces for potential publication outside of the classroom.

If students continue to revise their pieces for publication or submission to a writing contest, then the grade and the teacher's feedback attached to the grade can serve as one more round of revision before submission. Focusing on potential publication beyond the classroom also encourages students to consider what I like to call the "who would care" test where students pitch each other ideas and poll their classmates to see which of their ideas are most interesting among the group. When a student moves beyond just submitting a piece of writing to the teacher, then consideration of audience comes into play in a much more relevant way.

My favorite venue for students to submit personal essays and other creative work is the Scholastic Art & Writing Awards, which is organized each year by the nonprofit Alliance for Young Artists and Writers with Scholastic as the namesake sponsor. This contest starts at the regional level with multiple regions in most states across the country, and works that earn regional gold keys move on for national consideration. While earning regional or national recognition does not guarantee publication (though a number of regions put together publications of winning works, and there is the yearly *Best Teen Writing* featuring selected national gold key winning work), the contest offers a chance for gratification after putting in the hard work of writing. Since work is blind-judged, any work that receives high scores on the categories of originality, emergence of a unique voice, and technical skill can earn awards. There is not a preset number of awards like in a science fair or athletic competition. Along with the Scholastic contest, there are several other opportunities and venues for students to submit their writing listed in Appendix B of this book.

Regardless of whether or not they submit their work for publication, I try to remind students of the broader purposes of writing a personal essay. After they submit their final drafts, I ask them to consider what they learned about themselves, and also what they learned about others through the process of writing the essay. Some of my students' responses to those questions are featured in the "Student Snapshots" at the beginning of Chapters 4 and 5.

Sample Excerpts from Student Essays

After all the work students did with the activities from Part I of the book and then those from Chapter 4, my instructions to them for their final assessment are fairly simple:

> Write a personal essay or brief memoir (1,000–3,000 words) recounting and reflecting on a true and meaningful moment (or series of moments) in your life. Special attention should be given to two main components: story (narrative technique) and reflection (what did you learn about yourself, others, and or the world?).

Based on these instructions and having completed the lessons and activities shared in this book, my students produced a collection of excellent and honest work. Some of those essays are more personal and vulnerable than I'd be comfortable asking for permission to publish (though I know some of the same students submitted for Scholastic recognition and for publication in other venues), but Figure 5.1 includes three well-written excerpts representing the top-tier of quality from my students' work.

Figure 5.1 Excerpts from Students' Personal Essays

Three Mistakes in the Fall Line

I gave my father a thumb's up and listened to the chainsaw engine rev as my father pull-started the powerful 16" Poulan he used to cut down larger trees. My father let the engine run for a minute and then slipped his ear protection on before giving me the signal. As the come-along operator, I do not wear ear protection because I need to be able to listen for the tree to start falling and I am also far enough away that the engine's noise is not deafening. My father worked diligently for five minutes or so before he kicked the wedge out of the tree and signaled me to start cranking. The moment I started cranking was the moment I realized my first mistake. I put the hook lower on the tree than I thought, and that meant the come-along did not have as much leverage against the tree's inertia or resistance to wind. *Wind*: mistake number two. The wind pushed the top of the tree in the opposite direction from where I planned on falling it down. After slowly applying tension for a couple minutes, the wind picked up and the old rope visibly began stretching as the tree resisted the tension.

I called out to my father as loud as I could, but it was no use. His ear protection did what it was supposed to do and the Poulan had a very loud engine, which drowned out my screams even to my brother, who was standing about fifty yards to my right. I could not leave my post at the come-along, so I had no choice but to continue cranking. I took into careful consideration how much tension I applied to prevent the old rope from breaking with the wind blowing the tree around. I stared up at the menacing tangle of branches at the top of the oak. The tall oak, from base to tip, was at least forty yards tall, which meant that I had to run at least twenty yards to either side to ensure that I avoided the tips of the branches and the shower of wood chips that would surely follow the tree's impact with the ground. A few quick groans snapped my attention away from my calculations and back to the come-along. I heard a sharp crack, which meant the tree was about to come down, so I started cranking the come-along as fast as I could, putting my whole body into the motion.

A second, sharper crack brought all the nerves in my body to high-alert as the tree started leaning towards me. I would crank until the chainsaw stopped, the way I always did. I cranked furiously when a third crack ripped through the air, and I found myself lying with my face in the dirt and my legs fastened tightly together. A warm stream of blood rushed down my arm and my lungs gasped for air after the jolt of my ribs against a rock. I managed to flip over and I realized that the old rope broke about ten yards from the come-along and the rope whipped back and tangled around my legs. My hands quickly worked to untangle the rope as I nervously glanced at the tree. Several creaks audibly emitted themselves over the sound of the chainsaw, followed by a long groan and the very pronounced sound of cracking oak wood. The tall oak swayed dangerously in the wind and a finale of pops and groans erupted in my ears that made me realize my third mistake. The cracks I heard were not from the tree, but from the old rope. The chainsaw stopped.

There's No Place like Home

Sweat began to emerge from my palms as I glanced nervously around the room. My eyes shifted back down at the blank form on my desk that had been passed down the row to me fifteen minutes ago. The clock screamed at me as each eternal minute turned into the next. The questions were simple.

Name:

Date of Birth:
It was the next blank space that stopped me in my tracks.

Address:
I was the only student left with a form. I slowly scooted back my chair which made an eerie, noticeable noise. Slowly and shakily I laid the uncompleted form on my teacher's desk. I could feel the eyes of my peers burning into my back as I stood there facing away from them. I couldn't face them. A stinging sensation overcame my eyes as they began to fill with blurry sadness. Fight or flight kicked in and I ran down the hallway to the bathroom to be alone in my weakness.

My dad has been a pastor of the United Methodist Church for as long as I can remember. With the job comes a lot of moving. Every few years, the bishop of the district will match each pastor with which new church they believe will benefit most from their services, and moves them there. Every church has its own home in which their pastor and its family can live during their time preaching there. After five times around, I knew the system much too well. However, all of that changed when the sweet, old bishop retired and was replaced by a firm tyrant.

He came from Korea. His dark hair and rough skin with the look of a furrowed brow etched into his forehead were unfamiliar to me compared to the soft, gentleness of the last beloved bishop. The understanding and considerate eyes that once dictated the fate of so many pastoral families were replaced by harsh and fundamental ones. A smile never snuck its way onto his face, and he never showed any emotion. His mentality was to do whatever was necessary for the business aspect of the United Methodist Church to succeed. His voice and accent could shake even the bravest and toughest soldier. He was a snake that could kill and feel nothing. An uneasy feeling was always present around him, though I was secure. The last bishop had assured me that I could stay in my home town until I graduated, and a promise is a promise.

A Not So Haunted Restaurant Bathroom
I awoke to the sound of gentle rain pattering against the roof of our car. We arrived at an old brick factory building with floor-to-ceiling windows all the way around. "This must be the restaurant," I thought to myself.

"Dad and I used to go here a lot when we lived here," my mom informed us as we opened the double glass doors to the restaurant.

We sat down at a table in the back of the building. Lunch hour crowd filled the restaurant, occupying nearly every table. Our table had a bit of seclusion, and as we sat at the table, the commotion seemed to die down.

"I'm going to wash my hands," I told my mom as I got up and started to make my way across the restaurant towards the bathroom, taking note of the crowd of people and being careful not to be the cause of any accidents. I only had one collision today, and for the amount of incidents possible for that day I was doing pretty well.

I went into the bathroom to wash my hands, taking adequate time to apply soap and dry them. Pretty standard procedure. But as I opened the door to leave the bathroom I bumped head-on into a man entering. "That's two for today," I thought to myself.

"Hello?" the mysterious man asked into the bathroom.

But two people, upon running directly into each other, do not question who was there to collide with them. They promptly apologize to each other and continue on their way. This caught my attention, and I looked further into the situation. The man was taller than I was. He was bald, wore sunglasses, and was most prominently carrying a cane, waving it at the ground in front of him.

But this collision might have counted as more than one point, or less than one point, depending on how you look at it.

I just ran into a blind man.

I opened my mouth to apologize to the man, but something stopped me. I couldn't get myself to speak to this man. What could I do? I knew I should speak up and state my forgiveness to the stranger, but every time I opened my mouth, nothing came out. What was the worst that would have happened? I would have apologized, he would have forgiven me, I would have returned to my table, and the experience would have been lost to time.

But I didn't. I stood there in silence as a quiet ghost, haunting the restaurant bathroom.

Chapter

6

Masters of Truth: Interviews with Narrative Nonfiction Writers

Besides sharing my own ideas and activities for engaging students with narrative nonfiction in this book, I wanted to include the voices of writers who had earned success in the genre. The following interviews with professional writer MK Asante and student writer Johanna Bear demonstrate insight into both of their processes and showcase the benefits that each reports receiving from writing nonfiction.

I encourage teachers to use the perspectives and wisdom from these interviews to continue to consider the importance of narrative nonfiction in secondary ELA curriculum and to reflect on the usefulness of the activities presented in this book. If there are any quotes or advice from these interviews that might be useful for your students, please share them.

Professional Writer: MK Asante

MK Asante is the author of the best-selling memoir Buck, *for which he also recorded an original soundtrack and received a Sundance Feature Film Grant to adapt* Buck *for the screen (the film is currently in development). A multi-talented author, rapper, and filmmaker, MK is also a tenured professor of creative writing and film at Morgan State University. MK studied at the University of London, received a B.A. from Lafayette College, and an M.F.A. from the UCLA School of*

Theater, Film, and Television. While working on the prize-winning Starz TV documentary The Black Candle, *MK reached out to legendary poet Maya Angelou, who not only helped with the film but also became a long-term mentor. MK has lectured and toured at hundreds of universities across dozens of countries.*

I first met MK at the Baltimore Writers Conference, where he gave the keynote speech during the fall of 2014. "Talking to writers makes a difference in the quality of the conversation," MK said. As he talked about how, in Buck, *he weaved together separate layers including his own narrative, hip-hop lyrics, entries from his mom's diary, and letters his brother wrote from prison, I couldn't wait to read his book, which I picked up right after the session. After listening to the keynote, reading the book, and listening to the soundtrack, I knew I wanted to invite MK's words and wisdom into my own project. When I reached out to MK for a phone interview, he was enthusiastic about sharing his perspective with teachers and students.*

Jason Griffith: You're a multi-talented creative mind. You're a rapper, a musician, a filmmaker, you're a writer. How do all those different creative pursuits inform one another? How do they feed into each other?

MK Asante: How do they work together? You said it so beautifully, man. They work together in synchronicity. There's a lot of synchronization; it's like an ecosystem. But to me, all of those things are related, and they all really start from the blank page. Whether I'm working on a movie or a song or a book or an essay or even a speech or something, that's all going to be coming from the blank page. So, in a lot of ways, even though it seems like it's all these different things, to me, it's kinda not. They're very connected and related. They're all in the same family. They all inform each other.

And you said that, you said, how do they inform each other? Well, when I write prose, for example, because I'm a musician, the prose is rhythmic and musical. When I make music, because I'm an author, my music is literary. When I make movies, it has that literary/musical influence. So, it's like all these different mediums that I'm working in . . . other components and characteristics and techniques are coming out of those and feeding into the other ones. There's a lot of ideas in literature from music, and there's a lot of ideas in music from literature or film.

Griffith: What do you get out of writing memoir or nonfiction that you don't get from the other genres? What's special about memoir?

Asante: It's the most vulnerable. But I would say that, in a lot of ways, anything you write has elements of memoir. If you write a rap, and you talk about (breaks into lyric):

> *G-town, '98, me and my mother*
> *And mother-fuck the cops they knocked by brother*
> *He's State Road-in' it, 23 and 1*
> *Telling the time by the shadows of the sun*
> *My sis in psych ward, seeing strangers*
> *And I stay suspended—thug life behavior*
> *No savior, just danger, and pops left*
> *So now I'm gripping the banger*
> *Man of the house, North Philly to South . . .*

That's a memoir right there, you know? It's not formally a memoir, but there's elements of your autobiography in there. So, I think all work to some extent is autobiographical.

But, to answer your question, writing a memoir specifically in the style of *Buck*, for example, is the most vulnerable thing to write because you're putting it all out there for people to read and do whatever with. It requires, for me, the most mental and psychological work to put yourself out there like that. It's a lot different than, for example, writing a book about hip-hop. I'm connected to hip-hop. I love hip-hop. I am hip-hop. But, at the same time, writing a book about my mother and my brother and my father, that shit is all the way real. That's another level for me. That's one of the things about memoir.

The other thing about writing memoir is that it makes you reflect on your life in a way that you might not otherwise have. It forces you to think about who are the major players in your narrative? If forces you to think about what are the major transitions in your life and your story? What are the major turning points and the epiphanies? It really forces you to think about things in a way that, if not faced with the task of writing a memoir, maybe you would think about those things, depending on who you are, but maybe you wouldn't. Personally, I don't know if I would. So, I think memoir brings out a lot of deep introspection.

Griffith: That's great. That feeds into two of the other questions I wanted to ask you, with that idea of memoir being a vessel for self-exploration. When I work with my high school students in writing their own memoirs, I like to ask them afterwards, by going through the reflective process of writing the memoir, what did they learn about themselves, and what did they learn about others?

So, if I could ask you those two, starting with the first one. From writing *Buck*, what did you learn about yourself?

Asante: I learned that my upbringing really was like a village. What I mean is, when you reflect on your life in the way that I did, I just saw how so many different people in the village, my community, had so many different roles in terms of influencing how I think and who I am. It helped me acknowledge the village. That's how I would put it. It helped me acknowledge the village that raised me.

Griffith: You can really see that with you talking about your brother, and your mom, and your friends. They show up.

Asante: Yeah, my uncle and my teachers, you know, there's a lot of people that . . . even if it's just one line that they said to me or one quote that they gave me. All of those things come together and make up who we are.

Griffith: That's interesting. Some people who are critical of the memoir genre say that it's kind of narcissistic, but it almost sounds like, rather than just sharing your experience, you also used it as a way to give credit to those who have shaped you.

Asante: It definitely gives other people's perspectives, and obviously credit to those that were part of that village. And, I think that the memoir is not narcissistic at all. You want to write truth, and you want to write what you know, and, oftentimes, what we know is what we've experienced and what we've been through. And our truth is something that's directly related to our experience, and our vision, and our life. For me, writing memoir is really a way to connect to the world. It's a way not just to tell my story but lots of other people's stories.

But, when I say lots of other people's stories, I'm not just talking about folks in the village. When you write the truth and you tell your story, it's not yours anymore. We're all living in this world, and we're all experiencing these things. My memoir *Buck* is about mental health issues, it's about education, miseducation, re-education, self-education, street education. It's about rebellion. It's about literature. It's about writing. It's about reading. It's about finding your purpose. That has nothing to do with me. That has everything to do with me and nothing to do with me, you know what I mean? Those are things that we all can relate to and we all experience. So, writing memoir is really just a way to tell a lot of people's stories because everyone fits in.

Griffith: I think that's a great bridge to the second question. I remember at the Baltimore Writers Conference, you said you have a pretty good relationship with your dad now, but when you were writing the book, you actually re-experienced some of the emotions you did when you were young. So I'm just curious if you have any thoughts about what you learned about other people from reflecting and writing their experience. What did you learn about other people and the external world?

Asante: I think a lot of it is re-learning, and some of it is unlearning, rather than learning. It's like, ok, these are things you already knew, and then there's things that you have to unlearn. For me to write a first-person, present-tense, nonfiction story, you have to go there. You have to go to that place. You have to go to that space. You have to go to that time. You have to go through those emotions. That's definitely how I wrote and how I write. And that's why it's so taxing and emotionally and psychologically and physically draining to write memoir. It drains you in a way that, like I said, writing about hip-hop or something doesn't. And that's why I like writing about hip-hop too (laughs).

So what have I learned about other people? I learned that, while I was living my life and going through what I was going through, other people had their entire journey that was parallel to mine and intertwined but was completely different in some ways. I learned to see that, when I was doing this, here's what this person was doing, and here's what this person was doing . . . it gave me perspective on what else was going on at the time.

Griffith: Changing gears a little bit, one of, I think, your coolest stories is how you're working on a film, and you reach out to Maya Angelou, and not only does she want to help you with it, but she becomes a long-term mentor. I wanted to ask you specifically about that and some lessons you learned from Maya, and if you would use that to talk about the power of mentors in general?

Asante: Definitely. She's the reason why I try to mentor and help young people who are coming up. Because she did that for me. I remember when I showed up at her house, one of the first things she told me was, "I know you ain't got no money, so don't worry about it" (laughs). We were making this movie, and she agreed to help, and I flew out to Winston-Salem to work with her, and she was right. We didn't have any money. We definitely couldn't afford Maya Angelou. We definitely DEFINITELY could not afford Maya Angelou. But she said, "That's not what this is about." So, that was incredible.

One of the things she taught me that I thought was amazing . . . we were watching this documentary about her, actually, at her house. As we were watching it, there were some people making fun of her—like Saturday Night Live, Mad TV—that kind of stuff. Sketch comedy. It was kind of funny, but it wasn't flattering. And, she just started cracking up. So I started cracking up because it was kind of funny.

It just showed me that no matter who you are or how big you are, you're never too great to laugh at yourself and to have fun and to enjoy the human experience or the human experiment. Whatever you want to call it. And she told me to tell the truth when I write. She told me that if I do that, I don't have to worry about anything else.

Griffith: It's interesting when you said she's the reason you mentor, I noticed that when I was listening to the *Buck* soundtrack, there are so many times I heard you say, "He or she taught me . . ." or "This is where I learned this . . ." You kind of gave credit to folks who taught you lessons, and I was wondering . . .

Asante: Really? Like what? Do you have an example of that? I'm curious.

Griffith: You know, I haven't listened to it enough to quote the lyrics specifically, but I remember the track that Maya appears in, when you're introducing her, you say something like, "She taught me that . . ."

Asante: Oh, okay. Yeah.

Griffith: And there was another instance when you talked about your brother and you say, "He taught me that . . ." That was something that popped up again and again, those variations of the verb teach. Obviously, you're a professor now, so you are a teacher, but do you see your role as a teacher factoring into your creative work? Are those tools for you to teach and to share the lessons you've learned?

Asante: Yeah, definitely. And that starts with the blank page too, you know? I love being an educator. I love being in the classroom. I love being a professor, and I feel like, in a lot of ways, I teach what I do, and I do what I teach. So, it's all connected. That's something that I find very valuable. What I enjoyed about being at UCLA was that many of the professors that I had were working filmmakers, working screenwriters, working artists. So it wasn't like, "ok, this is all theory," or "this is what I think it's like." No, it was, "I just got off the set. This is how much we spent. This is how we got this done." You're getting the technical part of it and also getting their experiential stuff because they're living it and they're doing it. I think that's really important, especially when you're an arts educator. When you're in a creative field, it's important to have that knowledge and to be doing and to have that experience.

Griffith: I like that a lot, that idea of the teaching and learning go hand in hand with the doing. It's like that old cliché, those who can't do, teach. But, I agree with what you're saying. With the creative arts, I think it's so important that people teaching any kind of art are also working in it.

That's a great segue into the next question, which is, what advice do you have for other teachers? The audience of this book is middle school and high school teachers who will, hopefully, be using memoir and narrative nonfiction with their students, so what advice would you give them?

I remember the story in your book and also in your keynote at the conference about how, when you returned to school, your teacher told you to write and then didn't censor your words, but, in fact, she encouraged you. I remember you identified that as a big catalyst. So, what advice would you have for other teachers?

Asante: That's so big to me: autonomy and freedom of expression. Allow your students to create. Allow your students to choose, to dream. Allow them to think on the page. Allow them to challenge, and allow them to test and push the boundaries. Allow them to sometimes offend, because you won't always agree with everything they write.

I've spoken at jail, prison. . . . At a juvenile detention center yesterday, a guard asked me, "What should I do because these kids they write these raps, and they're so offensive, and they curse, and I shut them down because I just can't take it. It's so offensive."

So, I said, "First, you've got to understand that these young bucks are writing. They're creating. They're making poetry. Anytime you have someone writing and creating poetry instead of acting that out, and they're expressing themselves in an artistic way . . . number one, that's positive. Number two," I said, "if you would've read my shit when I was 16, you would have thought I was going nowhere too."

First of all, they're 16 years old. If you want them to write about more educational topics, then expose them to things. Right now, the kid she was talking about is 17 years old and is looking at 18 years in jail. What the fuck do you think he's going to write about? You think he's going to write about vacations to Martha's Vineyard? This kid, he's angry. He's got rage. He's mad, and that needs to be expressed, and we can't be afraid of it. We have to allow it. And, like I said, if we want the lyrics to change, and we want the content to grow and be more substantive, then exposure is the key. But not censorship, and not shutting that creativity down. When you shut that down, for so many people, that shuts it off for life, and they never get a chance to explore that and express themselves. So, freedom of expression is really important and also exposure to other literature and things that will inspire and inform the content.

Griffith: That reminds me of something you said at the conference. I can't remember if it was specific to a question that was asked during the session, or if you brought it up in reference to previous questions, but someone asked you about profanity and censorship. I remember you said that for *Buck*, you couldn't sanitize it to make it easier on the audience because it was your history. That sticks out to me. I think you used the verb sanitize. Does that sound right?

Asante: Yes, it does. Because our reality isn't sanitized, you know? Reality isn't sanitized. Tonight in Philly, a young kid is going to get his head blown off. That shit is not sanitized. Everyone is going to see that. His blood is going to be in the street. That's what happens. And it's going to happen in Baltimore and Chicago, and a white cop is going to shoot a black, unarmed person this week. This isn't sanitized; this is the world. This is happening.

Dr. Angelou told me one time, "Tell the truth. Now, when you tell the truth, you don't have to tell the brutal truth because the truth is brutal enough."

Griffith: I just have one more question for you, which is an open one, speaking directly to kids through their teachers who might pick this up. What advice do you have for middle and high school students who want to write about themselves?

Asante: It doesn't matter where you start, because you'll probably change the beginning anyway, but just start anywhere. Start somewhere. I would tell them one of my mantras; Eliminate distractions. Create positive energy. Fear absolutely nothing. And attack all opportunities. That's my advice for them as artists and writers.

But, they should not be afraid. Be fearless. Maya Angelou quoted the poet Terence to me. She said, "I am a human being therefore nothing human is alien to me." Nothing human is alien to us, so don't be fearful. Write your story. Write your experience. You matter. Tell your story, sing your song, and don't let anybody stop you.

Check out MK's books, music, films, and press at his website: mkasante.com

Student Writer: Johanna Bear

At the time of this book's publication, Johanna Bear will be beginning her freshman year of college. Despite still being a young writer, Johanna has already built an impressive résumé. As an eighth grader, Johanna's memoir Blueberry Whispers (2012) *earned a national gold medal in the Scholastic Art and Writing Awards along with the New York Life Award (a scholarship for works dealing with grief) and was published in* The Best Teen Writing 2012. *As a tenth grader, Johanna again earned national Scholastic recognition; this time a silver medal for her personal essay "Child of the Waves" (2014). As a junior, Johanna received an honorable mention in the* New York Times *Student Editorial Contest for her essay "Queers and Quads: Sexuality in Men's Figure Skating" (2015), and for over a year she has written articles and conducted interviews for Figure Skaters Online. During her senior year, Johanna earned national Scholastic recognition again, this time for a flash fiction piece titled "Paint Me by Numbers."*

I have had the great privilege to work with Johanna and her writing over the past 5 years. I first got to know her during her eighth grade year when she got involved with some writing workshops that I hosted at our middle school, and she also attended my summer workshop through the Capital Area Writing Project. When I moved to a high school position, Johanna was placed in my tenth grade honors English class, and she again signed up for a summer workshop that I hosted with a colleague at Dickinson College. While I've always been impressed with Johanna's innate talent, her versatility, and her drive, it has also been inspiring to watch her grow as a writer. Johanna sat down with me in person to share her experience and wisdom in an interview.

Jason Griffith:	You are a strong all-round writer. Besides memoir and personal essay, you write great poetry, and you're a strong academic writer. What do you get out of writing memoir and personal essay that you can't get from the other genres?
Johanna Bear:	Memoir is a really unique genre in that it combines so many elements of other genres. It reads like a short story and you can craft a narrative with different scenes, and you can also use beautiful, poetic language to bring out the emotional side of the story you're trying to tell. And you're also putting so much of yourself and your personal story into the piece.
	For me, it's always been the best of both worlds because I never felt confident enough in my imagination to craft a story that had no bearing in my own life, and I never felt comfortable enough with my language skills and my ability to stay within the parameters of poetry, even free verse. I struggled for a long time with being concise and narrowing down my ideas.
	With memoir, it combined all of the things I looked for in a genre. I felt true freedom to express myself emotionally and through my word choice.
Griffith:	It's interesting that you mentioned confidence. So you get confidence from the fact that the story has already happened, so you have a starting point, as opposed to free verse, where you might have the technical skills, but it's a blank canvas? So now you have this event that has happened that you can apply poetic language to.

Bear: Exactly. I've always struggled with being able to map out a story from beginning to end. When I try to write short stories, they always take a turn that I don't expect because I'm really bad at planning things out. Already knowing and having experienced the story makes it easier to literally pour your heart onto the page and to be able to take the core experience and then add literary skills to it and include the language and include the stuff that makes it more interesting and relatable.

Griffith: And it solves that problem for so many writers, which is "where do I start?" There are so many students who may have been told by their teachers that they're good writers, but they don't know what to write about. I think what you've already shared ties into the second part of this question, which is how does writing in multiple genres inform your memoir and essay writing process?

Bear: Recently, I've been working on a lot of poetry, which has helped me to become a more concise writer. I've always struggled in school when teachers impose page limits, and poetry has taught me how to tell a long story in fewer words and that each word that you choose and its location and the spacing, the formation of the stanza, even down to the syllable count—it all matters. It has made me more aware of the significance of every choice you make as a writer, and that awareness has helped my memoir-writing in turn because you become more aware of how the decisions you make as an artist affect your audience.

Griffith: Going back to eighth grade, you had some impressive success with "Blueberry Whispers," winning the New York Life Award and being published in *Best Teen Writing 2012*, but of course, that wasn't when you started writing. What led you to pursue writing memoir to begin with?

Bear: Honestly, it was having experiences worth writing about. Or, not even worth writing about, but having experiences that I wanted to communicate to an audience. The first memoir that I remember writing was about the loss of my grandparents' house. It was the first time I really experienced having an emotional connection to a place that I loved so much but would never be able to go back to because my grandparents were struggling financially and had to sell the house. I wrote it initially as a way of venting and getting it off my chest and examining my feelings because they were really complex, and I was unsure of how I felt about my grandparents' decision. Being able to lay down my thoughts on the page was a really therapeutic process of helping me understand where I was emotionally with the situation.

Then, I was able to share that with my parents to say, "Here. This is what I've been trying to say to you for the past three months."

Griffith: And you had failed to do that verbally?

Bear: Exactly. With writing, you have more time to sit down and really think through your emotions and think through all of the things that have been affecting you. Then, you can sort those thoughts to put them on paper. That was really important for me, and that was also the first piece that I submitted to the Scholastic Art & Writing Awards, in seventh grade, and I won a (regional) gold key. That was the first validation for me that my thoughts and my experiences did matter, in a sense, in a scope larger than myself.

That directly inspired "Blueberry Whispers" because it was a similar experience in that it was the loss of a house, but it affected me on an even more emotional level than the first house did because that place had been my safe haven for so long. As a young kid, you don't know how to sort through what you're feeling. As I got further away from the experience, I was able to come to terms with what I was feeling. The process of writing "Blueberry Whispers" was absolutely a therapeutic process. I remember sitting with my iPad and I wrote it all in one go, because it was venting everything, and it felt so good to get it out.

Griffith: You clearly communicated that, through the process of writing both pieces, you were able to work out experiences therapeutically. When did you start switching over and thinking that not only was this therapy for you, but it was also something that an audience could appreciate and connect to?

Bear: The first time I read "Blueberry Whispers" to someone, it was to my dad, who had been going to Yellow Shutters—the cabin that I had been writing about—since he was a child, and he cried. That was the moment when I realized that the piece had an effect larger than I initially thought it would, and that the themes of loss and powerlessness and helplessness are themes that everyone has to deal with in some form or fashion. Everyone has experienced being young and not understanding why decisions

| | are being made. That anger, frustration, and sadness are really common threads that everyone can relate to. |

Griffith: You writing about it, though you can't change the outcome, is in some way claiming some power over the experience?

Bear: Absolutely. And power in how I interpret it. Not just whining or saying "this is so unfair," but also saying, "I finally understand why this has happened, and I'm going to take this experience and become a stronger person because of it."

Griffith: Since "Blueberry Whispers" you've continued to have success both regionally and nationally with Scholastic and also nationally with the *New York Times* Student Editorial Contest. How have you grown as a nonfiction writer from eighth grade to now?

Bear: It's interesting. "Blueberry Whispers" and "Child of the Waves," which are the pieces that have been recognized nationally through Scholastic, are both about the same situation, but from different angles. "Blueberry Whispers" was about the house, and "Child of the Waves" was about me, and it was about how I grew as a result of the experience. As I've gotten older, it's that ability to be able to examine a situation from multiple viewpoints, rather than from a childish one of saying "this is the way it is" with no question.

Being able to look from multiple angles is an important life skill, not just a writing skill because not everything is black and white. In my writing, I've tried to explore different sides of something you might think is cut and dry, like with the *New York Times* Editorial Piece. Everyone thinks of figure skating as being a stereotypically feminine sport, but it doesn't support its athletes when they identify as gay. Looking at a situation that many people are familiar with but from a different angle. That's what's been the biggest staple of my growth, I think . . . the ability to not just see things one way.

Griffith: You probably realize this, but a lot of times we as English teachers force [students] to do assignments where you're basically writing out a long form of an answer that you already know. You're not really discovering something through writing. But, the most powerful experience in writing is when you learn something new as you go, and you don't know what the end point is going to be. So, in writing some of these editorials and these essays, what are some things you've learned about yourself through the process?

Bear: The biggest thing that I've learned is that I have an innate ability for empathy, which isn't something that can be taught. Like, through the piece that I wrote for Scholastic this year called "We Grow On," I look at my generation as it's been perceived through the media and by older generations. It's being able to take a situation like that that's very difficult to articulate and to try to put words to it.

I'm always doubting myself because my first success as a writer came unexpectedly and at such a young age. Every time I sit down to write, there's always this little nagging part of my brain that's not sure I can top what I've already done or not sure that I have the ability to continue writing at that level. If anything, I've learned that I really do have the ability to write consistently, and to write stories that people can connect to. I've always lacked aspects of self-confidence, and it's translated into my writing, but my growth as a writer is also my growth as a person. I've grown more confident in myself in all aspects of my life.

Griffith: In the same vein, what are some things you've learned about others and the way the real world works through writing your stories and personal essays?

Bear: It's going to sound so clichéd, but my writing has taught me that the world is a very complex place. When you think you know everything about a situation, about a person, about an event, you're only just scratching the surface. Being able to delve into specific moments in time through memoir, you realize things that you never would have thought you'd learn about yourself and the people around you. When you're writing about a situation with your friend, you can actually realize it's a really toxic relationship. Seeing things on the page makes it more universal and clear rather than just thoughts swimming around in your head.

Griffith: One of the things that a lot of creative writing teachers say at the college level, specifically with creative nonfiction, is that young undergrads usually write clichéd essays because of a lack of life experience. For example, I've read about the clichéd "dead grandma" essay, since the worst thing that's happened to a lot of young people is the death of a grandparent. What's your response to folks who would say that young writers can't write valid nonfiction?

Bear: It's difficult to stereotype and categorize writing or any other aspect of life because there are always exceptions. I don't think it's alright to say that there should be a minimum age for memoir because it's such a personal medium. It's almost like saying, "Your life doesn't matter until you get to age 30." You don't know everyone's individual experiences. Some young writers may have had experiences that even 40- and 50-year-olds haven't gone through.

I think the most impactful memoirs are written soon after an event because that's when the emotion is the most raw and the most tangible. There needs to be a period of disconnect so that it's not too cynical, but when you're just far enough removed that you can think logically about it while still feeling it. That's the perfect time to start expressing it through writing.

There are very young people who have experienced incredible and horrible things. If you lose or limit their voices, you're losing so much of the human experience. It's really narrow-minded to try to box in certain age groups as not being able to write meaningfully.

When I wrote a piece called "The Time-Traveler," and I read it at the Scholastic ceremony in Harrisburg, a woman came up to me afterwards, and she had written a letter to me while I was reading. The basic gist of which is that she had felt the same way that I had—out of place, disjointed, not connected to her age group—for her entire life, but she'd never been able to verbalize it. She connected to my piece on such a personal level, which really drives home the point that lessons that memoirs are trying to get at are so universal and so basic to the human experience.

Griffith: You make me think of *The Diary of Anne Frank.* I mean, talk about powerful nonfiction. She didn't really have the chance to reflect as an older person. And then there are the memoirs of the child soldiers: Ishmael Beah wrote one. Those are experiences that most adults don't have at 30, 40, 50, 80. Going back to something you said previously—taking something like your Maine house and how you wrote two different essays about the same thing from different vantage points. Chances are, when you're looking back at that at 30, 40, 50, the story will have changed to yet another vantage point, and you might not have access to that earlier lens. It may have expired.

Bear: When you write about something at a young age, you get a different voice than you would at any other time in your life. Using my mom's MS (multiple sclerosis) as an example, I'm going to think of that differently now than I will in 10 years. As a teenager, you're much more selfish, and you see only the disadvantages of it, and as you grow, you learn to live with that condition and how it affects your life but also how it affects her life. You get a much more mature vantage point. Being able to look at it from both angles, from both periods, is really important. It's acknowledging where you are, and it's almost like a time-stamp on what your emotional state is at a given time. That's a really cool thing.

Griffith: I like that. "An emotional time-stamp." Considering the writing experience that you have, what advice would you give to other teenage nonfiction writers?

Bear: The most important piece of advice I can give is that, regardless of what people tell you, your voice matters and your story matters. Whether other people have told you that it's irrelevant or that no one cares, people do care. There is a thread in experiences that can be relatable to all other kinds of people from all different walks of life. If you just have the courage to put your story out there, you'll be amazed at the places it will take you. It just starts with that first step.

Griffith: You mentioned courage and first steps. What about those first steps? What are some potential starting points?

Bear: I think the first step is figuring out, specifically, what you want to write about. You can't start with too broad of a lens. Narrow it down to a specific event, a specific moment in time, and take a tone of reflection, that's an important starting point. And then, it's such a cliché, but just keep writing. I have never been one for planning out anything that I write. I just sit and let the words flow onto the paper. I think that's when writing is at its most natural and its most effective—when you aren't worried about putting in a metaphor here, but you're worried about creating a raw, emotional experience for your audience. That's what can make it so powerful—it's that intimate connection between the reader and the writer.

Griffith: Considering that the main audience of this book is going to be teachers, what advice do you have for teachers who are trying to mentor their students to create the most evocative, honest, powerful pieces?

Bear: Not to discourage their kids because memoir can be a very revealing genre, and if you're discouraging them from a specific topic, it gives the sense that it doesn't matter or that their story isn't important. Even if it's the "dead grandmother" cliché, they're choosing to write about it because it is important to them. And, there's so much value to be gained from being able to put your thoughts, your feelings, your emotions, out there for other people. It's incredibly brave and it's incredibly important no matter what form it takes. So, I think not discouraging kids, especially ones who are just starting out, is important.

Griffith: What would you say is the role of trust between a writer and a writing teacher or mentor?

Bear: I think a mentor's goal should be to be there in any way that the writer needs. With memoir, it's not just technical writing, it's also emotional writing. Being there to help with the emotions of the situation for expressing those in writing, and then also the technical side. It's kind of part therapist, part writing coach. As I said before, it does take a lot to put your own experiences out there because it's not like fiction where you can mask your experiences behind another character, and you don't have to take ownership of that character's actions.

Griffith: There's a vulnerability.

Bear: Absolutely, the vulnerability of putting yourself out there as a character and saying, "This is me. This happened. This is true."

Griffith: Is there a formula that a teacher can use to guide a young memoirist?

Bear: Emotional connection + technical ability + courage = memoir success.

Griffith: So, I've asked you this list of questions. Is there anything else you'd like to say about yourself as a writer or about the genre?

Bear: Going back and looking at my earlier pieces, I can really see my growth, even from the technical side. I can see the arc of ability and age and experience, which is really cool. I can read myself growing up through my writing, which is a really special thing.

Another piece of advice I can add is that, in writing and in life, your failures can be just as impactful and life-changing and positive as your successes. One of the things I struggled with the most after my early success is that it wasn't immediately followed up. Having experiences of disappointment and feeling inadequate and feeling like I didn't have talent . . . I learned so much from that. It's an incredible lesson that writing in all forms teaches you. There is no clear cut, easy way to success. The story of writing is the story of rejection and pushing through until that moment of success. Through failure, you can learn a lot about yourself.

You can read Johanna's *New York Times* Editorial ("Queers and Quads: Sexuality in Men's Figure Skating") at http://learning.blogs.nytimes. com/2015/04/15/writing-for-change-student-winners-from-our-second-annual-editorial-contest/ and read her national Scholastic memoir entries at: www.artandwriting.org/media/44285 ("Blueberry Whispers") and at: www.artandwriting.org/media/159608 ("Child of the Waves").

Epilogue

Recently, I finished reading *The Other Wes Moore: One Name, Two Fates*. In this intriguing memoir, the author (one Wes Moore) examines his own life circumstances and upbringing in comparison with and in contrast to those of another man with the same name (the other Wes Moore) from the same part of West Baltimore. Besides their name and city, the characters share a number of other commonalities, but there's one key difference in their life trajectories. Just as the author was awarded a Rhodes scholarship, the subject was sentenced to life in prison for his role in an armed robbery where an off-duty police officer was shot and killed.

In his introduction, Moore (2011) wrote:

> Learning the details of his story helped me understand my own life and choices, and I like to think that my story helped him understand his own a little more. But the real discovery was that our two stories together helped me to untangle some of the larger story of our generation of young men, boys who came of age during a historically chaotic and violent time and emerged to succeed and fail in unprecedented ways. (p. xiii)

While the stark coincidence and contrast that Moore presents are, no doubt, unique, this quote presents a rationale for the value of reading and writing narrative nonfiction. Stories are how we make sense of the world. First, by reflecting upon, researching, re-contextualizing, and sequencing our lived experience in order to tell our own stories, we come to deeper understanding of those experiences. Such understanding is further enhanced when we hear and consider the personal accounts of others. We come to understand that our piece of the truth, although important, is relative and doesn't exist in isolation from other individual truths. All of our stories intersect, diverge, and mingle within a larger, ultimate truth.

Critics continue to minimize the value of personal writing both in education and in publishing. Just as David Coleman has professed not to care what students think or feel, there are writers and editors who dismiss memoir as self-centered navel-gazing. Granted, not all memoirs are created equal. There's a big difference between *The Diary of Anne Frank* and the latest Kardashian tell-all. However, as educators, we must first make our content relevant and interesting in order to engage students and maximize learning, and there's nothing more interesting to most of us than our own experience. And, with interest comes enthusiasm and investment, which makes it possible to move from "I" and "me" to "we" and "us."

When students are empowered to thoughtfully and responsibly tell their stories while also considering the stories of others, not only do they often craft important work that's of interest to readers, but they also reap academic, psychological, and social benefit. As Johanna Bear advised students in Chapter 6, "regardless of what people tell you, your voice matters and your story matters. Whether other people have told you that it's irrelevant or that no one cares, people do care." MK Asante echoed: "[D]on't be fearful. Write your story. Write your experience. You matter. Tell your story, sing your song, and don't let anybody stop you."

Appendix A

Reading Real to Write True

11 Tips for Teachers to Use Narrative Nonfiction in English Class

1. **Use mentor texts.**
Design nonfiction writing lessons around high-quality memoir, literary journalism, and essays.

2. **Not all memoirs are created equal.**
There's a difference between a ghostwritten celebrity tell-all and a thoughtful, researched personal account. Choose wisely and encourage students to do the same.

3. **Read like a skeptic.**
James Frey, Brian Williams, Stephen Glass, and Margaret B. Jones (among others) prove that it pays to read "truth" skeptically. Ask students to consider author credibility, narrator likeability, and trustworthiness of the account along with how these questions intersect.

4. **Use narrative writing to assess reading skills.**
What's better for evaluating student comprehension of literary elements like plot and character: a test/quiz, or actually having students apply these elements to an original narrative?

5. **Don't censor student writing, unless you have to.**
Empower students to tell their best stories (which aren't always pretty). If you have to censor, be up front and clear about why and under what circumstances.

6. **Consider timing.**
Traditionally, teachers have assigned a beginning of the year personal narrative as a "get-to-know-you" assignment, but students will likely be more honest and revealing after they've had time to build a trusting rapport with you and their classmates.

7. **Help them build the skills.**
What skills do you want students to master? Writing in active scenes? Using action and dialogue? Incorporating reflection? Embedding information and argument in story? Before you assign a personal essay, lead students through a series of mini-lessons to help them develop the skills you'd most like to see (remember to reference the mentor texts!).

8. **Give them (guided) time.**
Good ideas don't always come overnight (or at other predictable intervals). Give students time (along with guided brainstorming tasks and well-advertised deadlines) to find the right one.

9. **Do it with them.**
If you want students to write with openness and emotional vulnerability, demonstrate that you're willing to be honest and vulnerable by writing with them and sharing your work.

10. **Be mindful of sharing.**
Always give students an out when it comes to sharing personal writing. There's therapeutic value in personal writing, even if it remains private. Don't force students to peer-review or make their personal writing public without consent.

11. **All (good) writing is nonfiction.**
Whether it's a poem, short story or novel, memoir, editorial, research paper or instruction manual, all compelling writing has its roots in truth and lived experience.

10 Tips for Students to Write Engaging Narrative Nonfiction

1. **Capture your ideas over time.**
   Ideas don't come on demand. When you get a good one, be sure to have a collection method. Use a writer's notebook or an app like Evernote. Mine your social media accounts for stories that have meaning beyond that particular moment in time.

2. **Remember the advice of your mentor (texts).**
   Remember the narrative nonfiction book and other pieces you read? What did those authors do well? What do you want to try to incorporate in your own work?

3. **Tell the truth.**
   It's impossible to capture the whole (or ultimate) truth, so tell your relative truth and be faithful to your perspective.

4. **Do your research.**
   Look back at photos, interview others involved in your story, double-check verifiable details, and consider news and pop-culture from your featured setting. Getting the objective details right helps to build trust with readers when they get to your subjective experience.

5. **Write in scenes.**
   Good scenes have a start, an end, and a sequence from one to the next (like a movie).

6. **Write actively.**
   Including action and dialogue helps to put the reader in your shoes. Using active (rather than passive) voice helps to show rather than tell. Circle or highlight all of the linking/helping verbs in an early draft. Are there places which would work better with active verbs?

7. **Be honest and vulnerable.**
   Don't write for revenge or to settle scores, and don't write a story if you're not ready to tell it yet. That being said, honest accounts require thoughtful vulnerability. What do you have to admit (about yourself or others) to make this story work?

8. **Make an impression and leave an impression.**
   Invite readers in through intriguing first lines. Consider what story openings have drawn you in as a reader. Also, consider your closing lines. Can readers sense a shift? Have you arrived at the unspoken/unwritten ending line: "and nothing was the same after that?"

9. **Share your work with a friend.**
   Sharing work with peers allows you to consider how you're coming across and whether you're telling your intended story before you release it to the judgment of the world. Going public (especially with personal writing) is always nerve-wracking, so it's important to do it in increments.

10. **Write for more than a grade.**
    Consider writing for publication or for a contest like Scholastic. Doing so will help you reach the full potential of the piece. Often, graded drafts are good starts which could be even better with a little more work.

Appendix B
Narrative Nonfiction Resources

Creative Writing Journals Featuring Creative Nonfiction

- *Creative Nonfiction Magazine*: True stories, well told. www.creativenonfiction.org
- *The Sun*: Personal. Political. Provocative. Ad-free. http://thesunmagazine.org
- *Hippocampus Magazine*: Memorable creative nonfiction. www.hippocampusmagazine.com
- *Brevity*: A journal of concise literary nonfiction. http://brevitymag.com
- *Riverteeth*: A journal of nonfiction narrative. www.riverteethjournal.com
- *Fourth Genre*: Explorations in nonfiction. http://msupress.org/journals/fg/
- *1966: A Journal of Creative Nonfiction*. http://1966journal.org

Books on the Genre/Craft

- *You Can't Make This Stuff Up: The Complete Guide to Writing Creative Nonfiction from Memoir to Literary Journalism and Everything in Between* by Lee Gutkind.
- *Minds Made for Stories: How We Really Read and Write Informational and Persuasive Texts* by Tom Newkirk.
- *To Show and to Tell: The Craft of Literary Nonfiction* by Phillip Lopate.
- *Writing for Story: Craft Secrets of Dramatic Nonfiction by a Two-Time Pulitzer Prize Winner* by Jon Franklin.
- *Tell it Slant: Creating, Refining, and Publishing Creative Nonfiction* by Brenda Miller and Suzanne Paola.
- *Crafting the Personal Essay: A Guide for Writing and Publishing Creative Nonfiction* by Dinty Moore.

Personal Essay Anthologies

- *The Best Teen Writing* (Published yearly), includes national gold-medal winning works from the Scholastic Art & Writing Awards. More award-winning student personal essay/memoir can be found online at www.artandwriting.org
- *The Best American Essays* (Published yearly), Robert Atwan (Series Editor).
  - Guest Editors have included Ariel Levy, Edwidge Danticat, Cheryl Strayed, John Jeremiah Sullivan, David Brooks, David Foster Wallace, and others.
  - Also check out *Best American Sports Writing*, *Best American Travel Writing*, *Best American Non-required Reading*, and others in the broader series for more specific sub-genres of narrative nonfiction.
- *True Stories, Well Told: From the First 20 Years of Creative Nonfiction Magazine*, Lee Gutkind and Hattie Fletcher (Eds).
- *This I Believe Volumes I and II*, Jay Allison and Dan Gediman (Eds); archive of This I Believe essays (including those featured on NPR) can be found at http://thisibelieve.org
- *The Impossible Will Take a Little While: A Citizen's Guide to Hope in a Time of Fear*, Paul Rogat Loeb (Ed.).
  - Contributors include: Diane Ackerman, Sherman Alexie, Maya Angelou, Marian Wright Edelman, Jonathan Kozol, Nelson Mandela, Cornell West, and others.
- *40 Model Essays: A Portable Anthology*, Jane E. Aaron and Ellen Kuhl Repetto (Eds).
- *50 Essays: A Portable Anthology*, Samuel Cohen (Ed.).

Standout Narrative Nonfiction Podcasts

- **The Moth Radio Hour**: http://themoth.org
- **This American Life**: www.thisamericanlife.org
- **Serial**: http://serialpodcast.org
- **Radiolab**: http://www.radiolab.org
- **Snap Judgment**: http://snapjudgment.org

Student Writing Opportunities

- **Scholastic Art & Writing Awards**, Personal Essay & Memoir Category: www.artandwriting.org
- **The Norman Mailer High School Nonfiction Writing Award**: www.ncte.org/awards/nmwa
- **New Pages' Young Authors' Guide**: A comprehensive listing of student writing publications and resources: www.newpages.com/npguides/young_authors_guide.htm
- **The Adroit Journal Prizes for Poetry and Prose**: Secondary students can submit nonfiction in the prose category: www.theadroitjournal.org/adroit-prizes
- **Narrative Magazine High School Essay Contest**: www.narrativemagazine.com
- **Stage of Life**: Blogging, writing contests, and life for teens: www.stageoflife.com
- **Teen Ink**: Magazine, website, and books written by teens since 1989. Nonfiction category: www.teenink.com/nonfiction/

Appendix C
Common Core Standards for Reading and Writing Narrative Nonfiction

For this Appendix, I drew from the Grade 9–10 list of ELA Standards. Corresponding standards for Grades 7–8 or 11–12 would likely match the listed activities as well. Reading and writing narrative nonfiction uniquely satisfies Core Standards in Reading: Literature, Reading: Informational, Writing, and Language categories.

Activity	Standards	
Read and discuss a narrative nonfiction book.	CCSS.ELA-Literacy. RI.9-10.10	By the end of grade 10, read and comprehend literary nonfiction at the high end of the grades 9–10 text complexity band independently and proficiently.
	CCSS.ELA-Literacy. RL.9-10.5	Analyze how an author's choices concerning how to structure a text, order events within it (e.g., parallel plots), and manipulate time (e.g., pacing, flashbacks) create such effects as mystery, tension, or surprise.
	CCSS.ELA-Literacy. RI.9-10.3	Analyze how the author unfolds an analysis or series of ideas or events, including the order in which the points are made, how they are introduced and developed, and the connections that are drawn between them.
	CCSS.ELA-Literacy. RI.9-10.6	Determine an author's point of view or purpose in a text and analyze how an author uses rhetoric to advance that point of view or purpose.
	CCSS.ELA-Literacy. RI.9-10.8	Delineate and evaluate the argument and specific claims in a text, assessing whether the reasoning is valid and the evidence is relevant and sufficient; identify false statements and fallacious reasoning.
	CCSS.ELA-Literacy. W.9-10.9b	Apply grades 9–10 Reading standards to literary nonfiction (e.g., "Delineate and evaluate the argument and specific claims in a text, assessing whether the reasoning is valid and the evidence is relevant and sufficient; identify false statements and fallacious reasoning").

Activity	Standards	
List pre-reading inquiry questions; Read supporting nonfiction; Write a 1-1-1 research paper.	CCSS.ELA-Literacy. W.9-10.7	Conduct short as well as more sustained research projects to answer a question (including a self-generated question) or solve a problem; narrow or broaden the inquiry when appropriate; synthesize multiple sources on the subject, demonstrating understanding of the subject under investigation.
Contribute to collaborative chapter notes and class discussions.	CCSS.ELA-Literacy. SL.9-10.1	Initiate and participate effectively in a range of collaborative discussions (one-on-one, in groups, and teacher-led) with diverse partners on grades 9–10 topics, texts, and issues, building on others' ideas and expressing their own clearly and persuasively.
	CCSS.ELA-Literacy. SL.9-10.1a	Come to discussions prepared, having read and researched material under study; explicitly draw on that preparation by referring to evidence from texts and other research on the topic or issue to stimulate a thoughtful, well-reasoned exchange of ideas.
	CCSS.ELA-Literacy. RL.9-10.4	Determine the meaning of words and phrases as they are used in the text, including figurative and connotative meanings; analyze the cumulative impact of specific word choices on meaning and tone (e.g., how the language evokes a sense of time and place; how it sets a formal or informal tone).
Watch the film adaptation and compare/contrast with the narrative nonfiction book.	CCSS.ELA-Literacy. RI.9-10.7	Analyze various accounts of a subject told in different mediums (e.g., a person's life story in both print and multimedia), determining which details are emphasized in each account.
	CCSS.ELA-Literacy. RL9-10.7	Analyze the representation of a subject or key scene in two different artistic mediums including what is emphasized or absent in each treatment (e.g., Auden's "Musée des Beaux Arts" and Brueghel's "Landscape with the Fall of Icarus").
	CCSS.ELA-Literacy. RL.9-10.8	Analyze how an author draws on and transforms source material in a specific work (e.g., how Shakespeare treats a theme or topic from Ovid or the Bible or how a later author draws on a play by Shakespeare).

(continued overleaf)

Activity	Standards	
Write a personal essay.	CCSS.ELA-Literacy. W.9-10.10	Write routinely over extended time frames (time for research, reflection, and revision) and shorter time frames (a single sitting or a day or two) for a range of tasks, purposes, and audiences.
	CCSS.ELA-Literacy. W.9-10.4	Produce clear and coherent writing in which the development, organization, and style are appropriate to task, purpose, and audience.
	CCSS.ELA-Literacy. W.9-10.5	Develop and strengthen writing as needed by planning, revising, editing, rewriting, or trying a new approach, focusing on addressing what is most significant for a specific purpose and audience.
	CCSS.ELA-Literacy. W.9-10.3	Write narratives to develop real or imagined experiences or events using effective technique, well-chosen details, and well-structured event sequences.
	CCSS.ELA-Literacy. W.9-10.3a	Engage and orient the reader by setting out a problem, situation, or observation, establishing one or multiple point(s) of view, and introducing a narrator and/or characters; create a smooth progression of experiences or events.
	CCSS.ELA-Literacy. W.9-10.3b	Use narrative techniques, such as dialogue, pacing, description, reflection, and multiple plot lines, to develop experiences, events, and/or characters.
	CCSS.ELA-Literacy. W.9-10.3c	Use a variety of techniques to sequence events so that they build on one another to create a coherent whole.
	CCSS.ELA-Literacy. W.9-10.3d	Use precise words and phrases, telling details, and sensory language to convey a vivid picture of the experiences, events, setting, and/or characters.
	CCSS.ELA-Literacy. W.9-10.3e	Provide a conclusion that follows from and reflects on what is experienced, observed, or resolved over the course of the narrative.

References

826 Valencia. (2014). *642 things to write about: Young writer's edition.* San Francisco, CA: Chronicle Books.

Asante, MK. (2013). *Buck: A memoir.* New York: Spiegel & Grau.

Bear, J. (2012). "Blueberry whispers." *Scholastic Art and Writing Awards.* Retrieved from www.artandwriting.org/media/44285

Bear, J. (2014). "Child of the waves." *Scholastic Art and Writing Awards.* Retrieved from www.artandwriting.org/media/159608

Bear, J. (2015). "Queers and quads: Sexuality in men's figure skating." *The New York Times Learning Network Blog.* Retrieved from http://learning.blogs.nytimes.com/2015/04/15/writing-for-change-student-winners-from-our-second-annual-editorial-contest/?_r=0

Bernabei, G. & Hall, D.N. (2012). *The story of my thinking: Expository writing activities for 13 teaching situations.* Portsmouth, NH: Heinemann.

Bernstein, J. (2014). Jane Bernstein speaking at the 2014 Creative Nonfiction Conference in Pittsburgh, PA, May 23–25.

Blount, R. (2014). Still learning. In Bridges, L. (Ed.), *Open a world of possible: Real stories about the joy and power of reading.* New York: Scholastic.

Blumberg, A., Freemark, S., Kramer, S.K., & Richman, J. (2014, June 13). Seeing the Forrest through the little trees. *This American Life* [Audio Podcast]. Retrieved from www.thisamericanlife.org/radio-archives/episode/527/180-degrees

Bradbury, R. (1990). Run fast, stand still, or, the thing at the top of the stairs, or, new ghosts from old minds. *Zen in the art of writing: Releasing the creative genius within you*, pp. 13–30. New York: Bantam.

Brosch, A. (2013). *Hyperbole and a half: Unfortunate situations, flawed coping mechanisms, mayhem, and other things that happened.* New York: Square Peg.

Brown, B. (2010). The power of vulnerability. TED talk. Retrieved from https://www.ted.com/talks/brene_brown_on_vulnerability

Brown, B. (2012). *Daring greatly: How the courage to be vulnerable transforms the way we live, love, parent, and lead.* New York: Avery.

Cain, S. (2012). The power of introverts. TED talk. Retrieved from https://www.ted.com/talks/susan_cain_the_power_of_introverts?language=en

Cain, S. (2012). *Quiet: The power of introverts in a world that can't stop talking.* New York: Crown Publishing.

Coleman, D. (2011, April 28). Bringing the common core to life. [Speech transcript]. Retrieved from the New York State Education Department website: http://usny.nysed.gov/rttt/docs/bringingthecommon coretolife/fulltranscript.pdf

Collins, A. (2014, July 22). How playing an instrument benefits your brain [Video File]. *TED-Ed.* Retrieved from https://www.youtube.com/watch?v=R0JKCYZ8hng

Cooper, A. (2014, July 9). Anderson Cooper tries a schizophrenia simulator [Video File]. *CNN.* Retrieved from https://www.youtube.com/watch?v=yL9UJVtgPZY

Coulter, D. (2001) "Set 1: The young child's mind." *A guided tour of brain development.* [CD]. Longmont: Kindling Touch Publications.

Dean, D. (2006). *Strategic writing: The writing process and beyond in the secondary English classroom.* Urbana, IL: National Council of Teachers of English.

Dorfman, L.R. & Cappelli, R. (2007). *Mentor texts: Teaching writing through children's literature, K-6.* Portland, ME: Stenhouse.

Draper, S. (2014). My journey from reader to writer. In Bridges, L. (Ed.), *Open a world of possible: Real stories about the joy and power of reading.* New York: Scholastic.

Early, J.S. & DeCosta, M. (2012). *Real world writing for secondary students: Teaching the college admission essay and other gate-openers for higher education.* New York: Teachers College Press and Berkeley: National Writing Project.

Fassler, J. (2013, July 23). Why Stephen King spends "months and even years" writing opening sentences. *The Atlantic.* Retrieved from www.theatlantic.com/entertainment/archive/2013/07/why-stephen-king-spends-months-and-even-years-writing-opening-sentences/278043/

Fate, T. (2015, July 16). Rachel Dolezal's story? It's not creative nonfiction. *The Chicago Tribune.* Retrieved from www.chicagotribune.com/life styles/books/ct-prj-rachel-dolezal-race-white-lies-20150716-story.html

Foster Wallace, D. (2014). David Foster Wallace's syllabus for his 2008 creative nonfiction course: Includes reading list and footnotes. (2014, November 13). *Open Culture.* Retrieved from www.openculture.com/2014/11/david-foster-wallaces-syllabus-for-his-2008-creative-nonfiction-course.html

Gallagher, K. (2009). *Readicide: How schools are killing reading and what you can do about it*. Portland, ME: Stenhouse.

Gallagher, K. (2011). *Write like this: Teaching real-world writing through modelling & mentor texts*. Portland, ME: Stenhouse.

Goleman, D. (1995). *Emotional intelligence: Why it can matter more than IQ*. New York: Bantam.

Graham, S. & Hebert, M.A. (2010). *Writing to read: Evidence for how writing can improve reading. A Carnegie Corporation Time to Act Report*. Washington, DC: Alliance for Excellent Education. Retrieved from www.carnegie. org/literacy

The Guardian. (February 10, 2016). Retrieved from www.theguardian.com/ tv-and-radio/2016/feb/10/adnan-syed-serial-case-judge-defers-ruling-retrial

Gutkind, L. (2012). *You can't make this stuff up: The complete guide to writing creative nonfiction, from memoir to literary journalism and everything in between*. Boston, MA: Da Capo Press/Lifelong Books.

Hammond, W.D. & Nessel, D. (2011). *The comprehension experience: Engaging readers through effective inquiry and discussion*. Portsmouth, NH: Heinemann.

Hawking, S. (1996). Chapter 2: Space and time. *The illustrated a brief history of time*, pp. 22–45. New York: Bantam.

Hersey, J. (1946). *Hiroshima*. New York: Vintage Books.

Johnson, D.M. (n.d.). He said, she said. Dialog tags and using them effectively. *Scribophile*. Retrieved from www.scribophile.com/academy/ he-said-she-said-dialog-tags-and-using-them-effectively

Kerman, P. (2010). *Orange is the new black: My year in a women's prison*. New York: Spiegel & Brau.

Kidd, D.C. & Castano, E. (2013, October 13). Reading literary fiction improves theory of mind. *Science*, 342, 377–380.

King, S. (2000). *On writing: A memoir of the craft*. New York: Scribner.

Kittle, P. (April, 2014). Investment and independence: The superpower of story. *International Reading Association Secondary Reading Interest Group: The Exchange Newsletter*, 26, 4–5. Retrieved from http://pennykittle.net/uploads/images/ PDFs/PK_Writing/The-Exchange-Newsletter-April-2014.pdf

Kittle, P. (2008). *Write beside them: Risk, voice, and clarity in high school writing*. Portsmouth, NH: Heinemann.

Kleon, A. (2012a). *Steal like an artist: 10 things nobody told you about being creative*. New York: Workman.

Kleon, A. (2012b). Steal like an artist, TED talk. Retrieved from http://tedxtalks.ted.com/video/TEDxKC-Austin-Kleon-Steal-Like

Lamott, A. (1994). Shitty first drafts. *Bird by bird: Some instructions on writing and life*. Retrieved from https://wrd.as.uky.edu/sites/default/files/1-Shitty%20First%20Drafts.pdf

Lopate, P. (2013). *To show and to tell: The craft of literary nonfiction*. New York: Free Press.

Lopez, S. (2005, April 17). Violinist has the world on 2 strings. *Los Angeles Times*. Retrieved from www.latimes.com/entertainment/la-me-lopez 17apr17-column.html

Lopez, S. (2008). *The soloist: A lost dream, an unlikely friendship, and the redemptive power of music*. New York: Berkley Books.

Lopez, S. (2014a, October 11). Checking in with Nathaniel Ayers. *Los Angeles Times*. Retrieved from www.latimes.com/local/la-me-1012-lopez-nateupdate-20141011-column.html

Lopez, S. (2014b, April 22). No easy answer to the question of forcible medication. *Los Angeles Times*. Retrieved from www.latimes.com/local/la-me-0423-lopez-ayers-20140423-column.html

Lyons, S. (2013, April 11). Why Suzy Lee Weiss is completely wrong. *The Huffington Post*. Retrieved from www.huffingtonpost.com/sam-lyons/suzy-lee-weiss-wall-street-journal_b_3062517.html

Lyons, G. (2014, February 14). Creativity and madness: On writing through the drugs. *The Millions*. Retrieved from www.themillions.com/2014/02/creativity-and-madness-on-writing-through-the-drugs.html

Manjoo, F. (2008). *True enough: Learning to live in a post-fact society*. Hoboken: Wiley.

Mendelsohn, D. (2010, January 25). But enough about me: What does the popularity of memoirs tell us about ourselves? *The New Yorker*. Retrieved from www.newyorker.com/magazine/2010/01/25/but-enough-about-me-2

Moore, D. (2015). A genre by any other name. *Creative Nonfiction*, 56, 6–9.

Moore, W. (2011). *The other Wes Moore: One name, two fates*. New York: Spiegel & Grau Trade Paperbacks.

Morrison, T. (2015, March 15). Video: NBCC 2014 Awards Ceremony. *Critical mass: The blog of the national book critics circle board of directors*. Retrieved from http://bookcritics.org/blog/archive/video-nbcc-2014-awards-ceremony

National Board for Professional Teaching Standards. (2015, March 15). *Saturday 3:45 pm: America's best idea with Ken Burns, Johnathan Jarvis, &*

Milton Chen 480 [Video File]. Retrieved from https://www.youtube.com/watch?v=I0q8vlR1y6I

The National Film Board of Canada (NFB). (2014, July 17). Ladies and Gentlemen . . . Mr. Leonard Cohen [Video file]. Retrieved from https://www.youtube.com/watch?v=Uv4J7sID3Pk

National Governors Association Center for Best Practices & Council of Chief State School Officers. (2010). *Common Core State Standards for English language arts and literacy in history/social studies, science, and technical subjects.* Washington, DC: Authors.

Newkirk, T. (2014). *Minds made for stories: How we really read and write informational and persuasive texts.* Portsmouth, NH: Heinemann.

Newkirk, T. (2005). *The school essay manifesto: Reclaiming the essay for students and teachers.* Shoreham, VT: Discovery Writing Press.

Payne, S. (2015, March 20). Putting a "face" to a name: Students use FaceTime to meet author. *Periscope: The Student News Site of Carlisle High School.* Retrieved from www.chsperiscope.com/news/2015/03/20/putting-a-face-to-a-name-students-use-facetime-to-meet-author/#sthash.8DCZwenv.dpbs

Pennebaker, J. & Evans, J. (2014). *Expressive writing: Words that heal: Using expressive writing to overcome traumas and emotional upheavals, resolve issues, improve health, and build resilience.* Enumclaw, WA: Idyll Arbor.

Robinson, K. (2006). Do schools kill creativity? TED talk. Retrieved from https://www.ted.com/talks/ken_robinson_says_schools_kill_creativity?language=en

Robinson, K. with Aronica, L. (2009). *The element: How finding your passion changes everything.* New York: Penguin.

Rosenblatt, L. (1978). *The reader, the text, the poem: The transactional theory of the literary work.* Carbondale, IL: Southern Illinois University Press.

Rotten Tomatoes (2009). Retrieved from: www.rottentomatoes.com/m/soloist/?search=the%20soloist

Ryan, P.M. (2014) Stories of my imagination. In Bridges, L. (Ed.). *Open a world of possible: Real stories about the joy and power of reading.* New York: Scholastic.

Safer, M. (2009, March 22). Mr. Lopez meets Mr. Ayers [Video File]. *CBS.* Retrieved from https://www.youtube.com/watch?v=Kjr82pzrVSY

The San Francisco Writers' Grotto. (2011). *642 things to write about.* San Francisco, CA: Chronicle Books.

Sampsell, K. (2013). "I'm jumping off the bridge." In. C. Strayed (Ed.), *The best American essays 2013.* Boston, MA: Mariner.

Stein, J. (2013, May 20). Millennials: The me me me generation. *Time*. Retrieved from www.time.com/time/magazine/article/0,9171,2143001,00.html

Strayed, C. (Ed.), *The best American essays 2013*. Boston, MA: Mariner.

Ulin, D. (2010). *The lost art of reading: Why books matter in a distracted time*. Seattle, WA: Sasquatch Books.

Veselka, V. (2013). Highway of lost girls. In C. Strayed (Ed.), *The best American essays 2013*. Boston, MA: Mariner.

Watkins, S. (2009). *The young and the digital: What the migration to social network sites, games, and anytime, anywhere media means for our future*. Boston, MA: Beacon Press.

Weiss, S.L. (2013, March 19). To (all) the colleges that rejected me. *The Wall Street Journal*. Retrieved from www.wsj.com/articles/SB100014241278 87324000704578390340064578654

Wilson, T. (2011). *Redirect: Changing the stories we live by*. New York: Back Bay Books.

Woodson, J. (2014). *Brown girl dreaming*. New York: Nancy Paulsen Books.

Wright, E. (2004). *Generation kill*. New York: G.P. Putnam's Sons.

Yousafzai, M. & Lamb, C. (2013). *I am Malala: The girl who stood up for education and was shot by the Taliban*. New York: Little, Brown and Company.

Zacks, J. (2015, July 15). Why movie "facts" prevail. *The New York Times Sunday Review*. Retrieved from www.nytimes.com/2015/02/15/ opinion/sunday/why-movie-facts-prevail.html?_r=0